Lost in the Pages
a character's view of life

Gregory Smith

Thomas,
Thanks for being part of my life. You have been a blessing. The Author is bringing an extraordinary tale to life in you. Tell The Story,

Greg S

Black Lake Press
TELL YOUR STORY
BLACKLAKEPRESS.COM

Black Lake Press
TELL YOUR STORY
BLACKLAKEPRESS.COM

Cover design by Greg Smith of Black Lake Studio.
Author photo by Tim LaDuke of LaDuke Studios.

Published by Black Lake Press of Holland, Michigan.
Black Lake Press is a division of Black Lake Studio, LLC.
Direct inquiries to Black Lake Press at
www.blacklakepress.com
ISBN 978-0-9824446-8-9

Contact the author directly through his website:
www.smithgreg.com

To Linda, Andrew, and Maggie:

Without you, my story would be a tragedy, not worth telling.

Table of Contents

Author's Note

You will notice inconsistency in how the words *author,
story,* and *creator* are capitalized throughout this book. I
have taken some liberties to distinguish between storytelling, our little stories and the bigger stories into which
they are bundled, and my suggestion that we are living inside an actual Big Story, told by the Author and Creator of
the cosmos. My hope is that this will make the manuscript
less confusing, not more. You, the reader, will have to judge
whether or not this technique was successful.

G.S.

Part I

Stories All the Way Down

- chapter 1 -

Lost in the Pages

Much of the time, life looks like a muddled mess.

The weatherman forecasts, the bookie sets odds, the investor picks stocks. We plan our days, plan our weddings, plan our retirements. We set goals, cast visions, and write proposals. We place our trust in friends, our money in trusts, and our faith in God. We map out our vacations and educations. We build our careers and our homes, raising our children and our expectations.

When tomorrow comes, far too often we do not recognize it. It is nothing like what we expected. Despite all our efforts, tomorrow remains uncontrollable.

Our yesterdays are not much better. We try to remember and we try to forget. We try to explain how we got here, and we argue about how we did. We pick and choose our memories, forgetting what is not convenient and exaggerating what is. We remember ourselves as better than we were, and those who hurt us as worse. We are certain that we have not gotten what we deserve. We pad our résumés and will not talk about our embarrassments. Our recollections are fuzzy and we are blind to our biases.

And where are we, right now, in the landscape of life?

Like lost travelers, pointing at landmarks and stabbing fingers on maps, we are confused about the position and condition of our lives. We want to find the bright line that connects yesterday to tomorrow and understand where we are along it. Sometimes the landmarks look familiar and give us confidence. The next minute, they all look strange and we get the awful feeling that we have no idea where we have been, where we are, or where we are going.

Our metaphors set us up for this confusion. We describe life as a "journey," on which each of us tries to follow "God's plan for our life." We talk as if God has mapped a path for each of us through life's landscape, which we are to carefully walk along. So whenever we become bewildered about our journey (*What has happened to me? What is happening? or What might happen?*), we worry that we have somehow wandered off the "right" trail.

How could we have lost the road? Many Christians feel like we ought to have some sort of spiritual GPS that locates us within God's plan. We want to believe that our faith will track the waypoints of our journey, showing us exactly how and why the places that we have been are connected to where he is taking us next. We think, "Does being a follower of Jesus not mean that we march confidently behind him in life, certain of the path? How can the saved ever feel lost?" Panic sets in as we begin to doubt our faith, doubt our obedience, doubt our judgment. In our darker moments we doubt our salvation. In our darkest, we doubt God.

Maybe we have the wrong metaphor. Maybe life is not a journey along God's well-planned route. Maybe we are not following directions on what should be a safe trail to a secure destination.

Metaphors matter. They shape our perceptions, give us the vocabulary to describe our world, and are the slots into which we file our experiences. For example, because we imagine God as a king or a father, we behave in certain ways toward him. Those images shape our feelings about God, ourselves (we are subjects or children), and our response to him (we owe him obedience or grateful love). Of course, the Bible does use those metaphors; we did not decide to describe God as a king or father, *he* did (if you, as I do, believe that the Bible is God's word). He wants those metaphors to shape our feelings.

The Bible never describes life as a journey. In the New International Version of the Bible, the words *journey, travel,* or *trip* are never used in the context of a metaphor for our individual lives. "The journey of life," or some formulation of it, is not a biblical phrase. In four places, the New Testament uses "running a race" as a metaphor.[1] But the context of those passages seems to be that we should strive to serve Christ, not that God has issued us an itinerary. Metaphors do matter, and maybe we are using the wrong one. Perhaps that is why life so often seems muddled. If we imagine that our task in life is to carefully follow a route that God has mapped out for us, we will feel like failures when we lose the trail. We risk feeling abandoned, led into a wilderness without any clear instructions for what to do next.

But what if life is more like a *story?* What if God is like an author, and we are like characters in a tale that he is telling? What if we are living in a novel that has come to life?

Think about it: what are the essential elements of a story? There are conflicts and surprise plot twists. Protagonists and antagonists, each with their own character arcs[2] or threads, bump into each other. No one knows what is going to happen next, or why. The characters do not see everything, or know whether they are on page three or three hundred. Events in chapter seven might not be revealed as significant until chapter thirty-seven. The author drops clues and foreshadows what is to come, but the characters do not get to see where the plot is going, or how they fit into it. None of the characters know if they are the central protagonist, or just a supporting player. They *cannot* know those things.

To be fair, the Bible does not use story as a metaphor for life, either. But it does use *actual stories*. The Bible is a big story, containing lots of little stories full of all sorts of characters, and we learn what God wants us to know through them. At just the right point, God entered the story himself—as a character. We know very little about him, except what we learn through those stories. When he was on earth, he taught the people by telling them stories. Our sins are not forgiven when we grasp some theological proposition or sign onto some plan, but when we *believe a story* (the Gospel). We gather together and tell a tale about bread and wine, and we believe that acting out this story makes it become real in our lives. Want to know how the world ends? There's a story for that.

In the Bible, stories are the primary means that God uses to convey truth. Even in the poetic or prophetic books of the Bible, like Psalms or Isaiah, it is the stories behind the passages that give them context and meaning.[3] If we are going to pick some metaphor for life, let us at least pick one that resembles God's word. God likes stories, and he tells them so that we can learn about him.

Instead of being a muddled mess, our lives are baffling tales. They may be hard to understand, but they are not without direction and purpose. Instead of having lost some trail that we were supposed to be able to follow, we are characters in stories full of wonder and heartbreak, joy and tragedy. Our lives will only make sense in hindsight, as we see the threads of the narrative woven together and resolved in the final chapter. We are not lost on a journey; we are lost in the pages.

- chapter 2 -

Once Upon a Time

A traveler asked an Asian guru how the earth—the land and sea—is supported. "It rests upon the back of a great tiger," the holy man replied. The pilgrim asked what the tiger stands on. "The great tiger stands upon a great elephant." But what does the elephant stand on? "Upon the back of the World Turtle." The traveler persisted: what is under the turtle? "After that," said the guru, "it's turtles all the way down."

Your life is a story. That story rests upon (or inside) another story. After that, it's stories all the way down, until we get to the Author. 4

God has a plan for your life, right? Most Christians would say that he does (and so would most Jews, Muslims, and a host of other folks who believe in some sort of higher power, destiny, or fate). But what do we mean by that, exactly?

We usually think of God as having two different types of plans for our lives. The first is a set of general prescriptions for various aspects of life: "God's plan" for marriage, child rearing, financial management, business, health, evangelism, church growth, etc. Supposedly, if these principles or actions are carefully followed, then the result will be a successful home, church, business, body, or bank account.

We also think of God as having an individual blueprint for each of our lives, with our challenge being to figure out this "plan" and stick with it. If we can interpret and follow his instructions (for where we should go to school, whom we should marry, what we should do for a living, where we should live, what church we should to go to, etc.), then we will "fulfill God's plan for our lives." It will turn out well for us.

There are two little words embedded in both those ideas: *if* and *then*. They form a logical promise: if we do *x*, then *y* will result. This is a mechanistic view of the universe that requires experts who have learned its laws and formulas. And so we approach all of life like it is medicine or engineering. We consult Christian experts to learn how to put together a successful life or how to fix a broken one. Do you want a happy marriage? Good kids? Enough money? A bigger church? There's always some expert who will tell you that *if* you use this key, follow these steps, or implement that program, *then* things will be bigger and better. The premise is that the right plan guarantees right results because it is derived from spiritual laws and observable principles—like science.

Our goals are sincere and practical. We want a happy family, good health, prosperity, and other tangible blessings. People everywhere have always wanted these things. Most religions have prescribed plans to achieve them, from sacrifices to rain dances to holy wars.

But what if things do not work out like we expected?

Then what? What if we follow the program, take the steps, and implement the key principles and our marriage still fails, our kids still grow up rotten, we still go broke, and our church still shrinks? What happened?

When our efforts to follow God's plans go awry, we usually assume that we must have done something wrong, or bad. Either we missed a step somewhere, or we followed all the steps but some secret sin has put us onto God's naughty list. In either case, we assume that it is somehow our fault. Again, there is no shortage of experts (like Job's friends, whom we'll talk about in chapter seven) to point out another set of if-then laws to us: if things went badly, then we must have done something to cause it.

After all, Christianity is supposed to "work," right? Is the outcome not supposed to be the right kind of life? And so some of us approach the Christian life as if we are assembling a kit. Imagine that you want to build a garden shed. The truck from the building supply store unloads a pile of precut lumber, shingles, and hardware onto your driveway. You pour over the plans: twenty-seven pages of parts lists and instructions. *If,* when you are done, the door hangs the wrong way and you have leftover parts scattered on the driveway, *then* you must have misread, misunderstood, or just outright missed a step somewhere. Some of us approach life the same way. Our mechanistic view of the universe demands that we be able to trace every effect back to some cause. We search for life's instruction manual, and assume that those who struggle must have not followed it properly.

But generally, the Bible does not describe life as a plan

to be followed. While that word does occur a handful of times in the context of God's plans for his people as a whole,[5] it is never applied to an individual in the sense that we use it today, as "God's plan for my life." The Bible does talk quite a bit about men's plans for their future, usually to point out that they are shortsighted or misguided. It does tell us to follow God's laws, but that is a very different concept. Our culture is big on God's plans, not so much on his Law.

I do not think that God has a *plan* for my life. I think that he is telling a *story* through it. Stories are not like plans. They are not blueprints for life. They contain no instructions in which connecting Part A to Part B in Step Four leads to the assembly of Unit C in Step Nine. Stories do not work that way.

Stories always have certain elements: conflict, protagonists and antagonists, plots, plot twists and subplots with twists, minor characters, foreshadowing, settings, and surprise endings. The characters think and dream, will and choose, act and interact with each other, but they are carried through and tossed about inside a bigger structure that they can never step back far enough from to completely understand.

God likes stories. He is the Author of the greatest story ever told. To understand it, let us imagine it as a novel—or even better, as the movie version. If the Bible were a novel or a movie, what would be the opening scene?

According to the first two chapters of Genesis, it would be a bright new world, hanging in a bright new universe. Infant galaxies glisten, blazing with primordial flame. Our planet spins through the juvenile heavens. All is right between the Creator and humanity, between man and woman, and between the two of them and the Creation. It is all good. Very good.

Stories often begin by laying out the setting and the characters and then the conditions that will move the narrative forward. Therefore, in the third chapter of Genesis, an if-then condition is introduced. It is nothing less than the device upon which the entire plot hangs: *if* they eat of the Tree of Life, *then* they shall surely die.

Then we meet another character. The serpent is more crafty than any of the other animals. He exposes human motivations that were hidden and stokes them into action. He introduces internal and external conflicts. He twists the plot by twisting the if-then condition. "When eat from [the fruit]," he tells Adam and Eve, "your eyes will be opened, and you will be like God, knowing good and evil."[6] The universe holds its breath, hanging on every word of the story, every movement of the characters. Then the woman plucks the fruit. She gives some to her husband who is standing there, apparently mute, and they eat it. The universe shudders. The angels in the audience gasp. Something snaps.

From that moment, the creation has been broken. Our DNA has carried a congenital defect. We are not now as we were made to be. We see through a glass, darkly. The things we do not wish to do, we keep on doing. We die. We not only broke ourselves, but we broke the universe as well. It has been infected with our disease, as if at the molecular level. In his letter to the Romans, Paul describes its "bondage to decay" and its "groaning," and says that it is "waiting in eager expectation" to be "liberated" when we are, someday, healed.[7]

If the Bible were a novel or movie, what would be the closing scene? The opening scene was described in the first two chapters of Genesis. The final scene of the Bible story is described in the last two chapters of Revelation. The Bible is bookended by these two scenes.

And guess what? The last scene looks very much like the opening scene. There is a new heaven and a new earth, with peace between God and man, between man and woman, and between them and the Creation. There are now many Trees of Life, lining Main Street in the City of God, bearing fruit for "the healing of the nations."[8]

Thus, the Bible ends as it began. It tells the Big Story[9] of how the universe gets from the first two chapters of Genesis to the last two of Revelation. It moves, in classic three-act storytelling format, from exposition to conflict to resolution.

Inside this Big Story there are many small stories: humanity tries to build a tower, a man builds an ark, a barren woman is promised a child after she dedicates him to the Lord, a boy is destined to be king, a king squanders his success by taking another man's wife and murdering her husband, a man is lowered in a basket from hostile city walls, a boy has a few fish and loaves, a man leaves his tax booth, a woman pours expensive oil onto the feet of a stranger who knows her better than she knows herself, and then washes them with her tears and hair.

Like so many great stories, this one has an unexpected twist. The Author writes himself into his own tale as a character, and becomes the pivot upon which the whole thing turns.

And when the Author of the Story and the stories was on the stage himself, he taught us with stories. He knew their power, that sometimes we cannot remember the point of a sermon but can remember the stories the pastor used to illustrate it. He knew that stories can bypass our rational mind to directly affect our heart. He knew that stories can shift our center of gravity and alter the trajectory of our lives.

God likes stories.

Our individual stories take place inside this Big Story. We are characters, each of our lives intersecting and playing a part in each other's story, fitting into and intersecting with even bigger stories, which are subplots of bigger stories yet, spanning generations and continents, races and empires. We are woven inextricably into comedies and tragedies and morality tales that we can never step back far enough from to completely see the whole.

Yes, God is the great teller of tales. True tales. The world is like some wondrous novel, with billions of characters and billions of subplots, a place where every door leads you higher up and deeper into new rooms and glens and glades in a sprawling forest full of sadness and surprises and joy (both real and just hinted at like buds in spring). Like the characters in Chaucer's *The Canterbury Tales*, we are on a pilgrimage, and as we travel we tell each other ourstories. Except that ours are real, and connected like a vast, living thing.

It's stories, all the way down.

- chapter 3 -

A Storied Cosmos

It is only fair for us to fly our flag when we talk about important things. We should be honest about our prejudices and loyalties. Impartiality is a myth: none of us comes to any significant conversation without a perspective on the world, what might be called a *worldview*. Here is mine: we live in a storied cosmos.

I must admit that I've always wanted to see the world in a sweeping, literary way. I've always been enchanted by the grand scope of the universe, by the intricate sprawl of porpoises, poetry, and the Pleiades. Consequently, I've been a sucker for any sort of grand unification theory that could make sense of it all.

So I was impressed by a television documentary series I saw in college. It was called *Cosmos,* a fusion of science, history, and 1970s pop philosophy, written and presented by the astrophysicist Carl Sagan.[10] It was an imaginative, witty, and visually creative presentation of a particular worldview: that the cosmos is, as Sagan put it, "All that is, all that ever was, and all that ever will be." He pointed out that our bodies are built from molecules manufactured in the hearts of stars. As Sagan famously intoned, "We are star stuff which has taken its destiny into its own hands."[11]

Unfortunately, *Cosmos,* and the worldview it so cleverly captured, is profoundly mistaken. It creatively and lyrically connected wonderful data to mistaken premises and thus arrived at bad conclusions. I appreciate the insights, but in the end I do not recognize the cosmos it describes.

Everyone has a worldview, although most of us struggle to articulate it. It is like trying to explain your language, or your hearing, or what the color green looks like to you; it only makes sense when we compare it to someone else's. Expressing our own worldview takes exposure to other belief systems and effort to unpack the differences.

A worldview is not the same thing as a religion. In one sense a religion fits inside of a worldview. For many reasons, I believe in a universe in which God is not only *possible,* but also *probable.* Because I think that I live in that type of cosmos, I have to make decisions: which god? What holy book? Whose faith community? How should I worship? My worldview creates a space which my religion fills.

In turn, my religion also affects my worldview. My Christianity colors my view of everything, not just religious things. Because I believe the story that historic Christianity tells, I must also believe—if I am to have any intellectual integrity—certain things about the physical universe and animals, about money and marriage.

I want my worldview to have integrity, for it to be a holistic approach to faith and science, theology and philosophy, politics and business. That feels hard to do in the early twenty-first century. We have built fences between our science and our faith, between the practical and spiritual. The older I get, the more false those distinctions seem to me. I see multicolored galaxies and an island with a thousand shades of green. I hear a girl crying because a puppy that she saved for months to purchase—and fiercely loves—is missing. I hear a gypsy's well-worn plea on a Paris street. I taste a moment from the Highlands, captured eighteen years ago in a bottle of single malt scotch. I feel the stress of earning enough to support my family. In all of these, I hear stories. Big and little stories that form the interlaced structure of our universe, all of them hints and invitations and gateways to the great narrative arc of the cosmos.

Sagan was right about our bodies. We are star stuff, but we are star stuff that was breathed into by the Author and became alive. I see a universe that seems more written than random. Everywhere, I see narrative movement: from some sort of a beginning, through a middle, to some sort of an ending. Throughout history, people have sensed that we are part of some larger story and speculated about the *what, when, how* and—most importantly—the *why*. It feels like it all has some purpose, but we cannot figure out what that purpose is. The universe moves from event to event, the characters are small but important, and every page reveals some new, hidden connection. But to what end?

People with Sagan's worldview like to say that we are an insignificant species, on an insignificant planet, circling an insignificant star on the outer ring of an insignificant galaxy in a vast cosmic sea. How do they know that? What makes our position in the universe so insignificant? Is our planet less important because it is *smaller* than others? Because it is not aligned symmetrically on the galactic map? Because ours is only a tiny fraction of the total number of solar systems?

What some see as statistically insignificant, I see as intriguing. What some see as an accident of space and time, I see as a curious tale. What they see as an ultimately pointless evolution of star stuff, doomed by the eventual flaring out of our sun, I see as the tension of a big story, building to a hair-raising and potentially disastrous ending. I cannot wait to see how the Author ties all these loose ends together.

We are not the central characters in this Big Story. According to Christianity, God is the central character in three ways: he writes himself into the story as Christ, he is the primary actor in history as the Holy Spirit, and it all adds glory to the Father, the Ancient of Days. Of course humanity is a critical part of this tale. In *The Iliad*, Helen of Troy is the proximate cause of the war, and the sulking of Achilles is its central drama, but it is not about either of them. Like them, we may be featured in the Big Story, and the Bible tells it from our point of view, but it is not about us.

There are elements of this story that we cannot see, at least not yet. In novels, characters in one chapter are often unaware of the existence, much less the actions and purposes, of characters in some other chapter set in another place or time. In the same way, there are characters in this story that we have not yet met. Some, but not all (and maybe not even most), of them are human; there are angels and demons and leviathans in the deep. If we catch glimpses of them from time to time, we can only speculate at their role and arc in the Big Story, and where and when it might intersect with ours. Perhaps, when and if all the other characters and settings and plots are revealed, our and our planet's place in the cosmos will make more sense.

The Big Story has all the elements of a good tale: conflict, redemption, plot twists, etc. Maybe that is why we like stories so much, and why they mean so much to us. The reason we appreciate color and sound is because we were made to live in a physical universe of vibrations and electromagnetic waves. Our senses are attuned to them. We were created from this storied cosmos and designed to live in it. A good story vibrates our bones at their resonant frequency. Like fish are made to live in water, we were made to be characters. Because narrative is bred in our bone, we are drawn to myths. We cannot explain the thunder so we invent Zeus; we cannot explain what holds the earth up in space, and so we imagine the World Turtle.

Perhaps Christianity is just another mythic tale, told to fill in the gaps in our understanding. Some Christians have begun to embrace the notion that the mystery and wonder of stories is more important than whether the stories are true. Therefore, it would not matter whether Jesus really rose, or even whether he really lived. Similarly, they believe that it would not matter whether God created Adam and Eve without disease or death, or whether Christ really will return to remake the heavens and the earth before our star dies out like a campfire at dawn. The important thing, according to this way of thinking, is that the story inspires and motivates us. They argue that the purpose of the biblical tales is to draw us into some inscrutable mystery or mystical truth.

Do not misunderstand the point of this book. When I say that God is a storyteller, that the Bible is a collection of stories, and that our lives and world are a Big Story, I do not mean that they are merely stories. I do mean that we perceive God's actions as stories. Maybe a better way to say it would be that the format of a story best resembles how the universe works, more than a plan or lecture or any other medium. God created a universe with conflict, in which events unfold and build on each other in causality and significance. God the Father does not observe his creation in linear sequence, but we do. He reveals what matters to him in the playing out of all these events, and we discover his will as the pages turn. We experience life more like characters in a story than as scientists evaluating data, or as builders scanning blueprints. We do not stand back and appraise what God wants us to learn; we discover it as we live it out. As Proverbs 20:24 observes, "A person's steps are directed by the LORD. How then can anyone understand their own way?"

Living in a storied cosmos means seeing and understanding our lives in particular ways. It means that our lives are not random, but that from our vantage point they are unpredictable. It means that conflict, hardship, and suffering might be the essential elements in our lives, not necessarily signs that our lives are off track. It means that some, maybe even much, of what is important happens out of our sight, and that this a feature, not a flaw, of life. It means that it is not all about us. It means that we are all going somewhere and becoming something. It means the only way we will learn where and what is to watch and wait.

- chapter 4 -

And Thereby Hangs a Tale

I wrote the last chapter in a coffee shop near the college in the town where I live. As I was writing, a man and woman came in and sat a nearby table. Little, steamy clouds rose from their mugs. The man sipped at his as he read the newspaper.

She was tall. Her dress and demeanor were well composed. As the man read, she sat up straight, neither reading nor drinking her coffee. She just stared off into the middle distance. After a bit, she began to cry. Not loudly or demonstrably, but quietly. She was struggling to maintain her composure. Neither of them spoke. He kept on reading his paper. This went on for some time, until he looked at her and said something like, "You ready?" She said nothing, but they stood, put on their coats, and walked out without any more words between them.

Who were they? What was going on in their lives? I sat, speculated, and invented possible stories to explain the scene. In truth, I felt like a coward. I thought that perhaps I should have asked if they were all right, or if they needed any help. Unemployment has hit my town hard over the last couple of years, and many folks have lost their homes or suffered other hardships. I have friends—more caring and outgoing than me—who might have spoken up and reached out to them. Me? I did what I far too often do: watched and speculated and theorized. I do not know what their story was, but I know that there was a story—maybe a powerful one—that explained what happened that morning.

Ernest Hemingway developed an especially lean storytelling style, described as being all verbs with no adjectives. Supposedly, some of Hemingway's drinking buddies once bet him ten dollars that he could not write a novel with only six words. He took the bet. A couple of days later, he came back and presented it to them. He had written, "Baby shoes. For sale. Never worn." His friends paid up, because contained in those few words is a universe of possibilities: characters, hope, unforeseen events, pain, desperation, turns of fate, and changes of direction.

Life is full of moments which open doors for us to listen to, learn about, and live within each other's stories. Stories ask questions which usually raise more questions, which lead to more stories and more questions. Those become portals and wormholes to even more stories. If there really are only seven degrees of separation between everyone on earth, then our stories all begin to intertwine at some point. Every day is a new opportunity to discover something awful or wonderful, to meet other characters which connect the subplots and foreshadow future events. As William Shakespeare wrote in *As You Like It,*

It is ten o'clock...'how the world wags:
'Tis but an hour ago since it was nine,
And after one hour more 'twill be eleven;

And Thereby Hangs a Tale

And so, from hour to hour, we ripe and ripe,
And then, from hour to hour, we rot and rot;
And thereby hangs a tale.[12]

The rapid-fire details of life—from crying women to lost car keys to failed math tests to used items for sale in a classified ad—are the stuff of our stories, and on them hang our tales.

Reflecting on how stories work might suggest ways to make sense out of our lives. At its core, a narrative has a character, and that character acts and interacts with other characters. Even if the character is not human, it still must interact, have some arc of development against conflict and over time. A rock that just lies on the ground, doing nothing, is not a story. But a bit of pollen carried by a bee, tossed by the wind, and against all odds growing into a flower in a faraway meadow is a story. A fish swimming in a fishbowl is not much of a story, but *how* the fish ended up in captivity, its relationship with the owner who feeds it, and its eventual fate, might make a great tale. Stories involve things like exposition (describing who the characters or other elements are, or how they got that way), plotting (what happens to them over time), conflict (the problems they must solve), and resolution (how the problems get solved—for better and for worse).

In good storytelling, characters and events are not merely random occurrences. They may appear to be random—for a while. Eventually, it will be revealed that they had always been part of a purposeful and developing narrative. The crying woman, the advertisement for baby shoes in the newspaper that the man in the coffee shop is reading, the cowardly writer at the next table, the man in the brown fedora removing his raincoat by the door, and the bomb that exploded yesterday on the bus in Marseilles: they all *seem* to be random and disconnected. In the hands of the Author they fit into some bigger movement, even if all those characters never grasp it. People and events matter. We are not portraits hanging in God's gallery, nor plants in his garden: we are his prodigal children finding our way home, discovering his restoration of the cosmos as we live it out and act within it.

The Greek philosophers Plato and Aristotle, living in the fourth century BC, pointed out that an author might tell his story through one of two perspectives. The author might adopt the voice of an invisible narrator who stands outside the story (for example, "Achilles then sprang upon the Trojans with a terrible cry, clothed in valour as with a garment."[13]). Plato called this *diegesis*. On the other hand, an author might choose to describe events or share his own viewpoint through the voices of characters within the story, which they called *mimesis*.

So how does the Author of our cosmos tell us stories? As far as we can tell, there is not much external narration. The Bible does contain some chapters told in the voice of the omniscient narrator: the first chapters of Genesis, some chapters in Revelation,[14] a handful of critical verses in the book of Job. Sometimes—but not very often—the perspective widens and we see outside of this world. But most of the Bible is told from a human vantage point, from inside the confines of the bigger story of human history. Many of the biblical books are written by people who themselves occur in the narrative of the Bible. Granted, some are anonymous, but even if we argue about the identities of the authors, the vantage point and the narrative voice is earthly (within the story), not heavenly or otherworldly. The Books of Moses and the histories of Israel are seen from the perspective of the characters. The Psalms and other "wisdom books" are the voice of David or Solomon or their collaborators, and certainly come from a human vantage point. The prophetic books are the voice of the prophets, who are themselves characters in the story. The entire New Testament is told from the perspective of characters within the story; the apostles relate stories of Jesus and write letters of instruction and advice to the early Church. Jesus himself is a classic example of the Author sharing his thoughts through a character within the story; God becomes a man and speaks his mind within history, which is recorded by eyewitnesses who write accounts of both Jesus' actions and theirs.

Film students learn two ways to use music within a movie. The most common is as a song or background score, played over the action. It is for the audience's benefit; the characters do not hear it being played. On the other hand, a song might be played, or sung, or merely heard, by a character inside the film; it exists within the world of the characters, and they hear and are affected by it.[15] Musicals all use this technique; the characters sing to each other, and the songs arise out of and advance the action. It is used in dramas, as well. Remember *As Time Goes By*, the song made famous in the classic 1942 film, *Casablanca?* In one of the most iconic scenes in movie history, Ilsa (Ingrid Bergman) is sitting next to Sam (Dooley Wilson) in Rick's Cafe, begging him to play the song that he had played so often for her and Rick (Humphrey Bogart) in Paris before the German invasion. To keep him from remembering Ilsa, Rick had forbidden Sam to ever play *As Time Goes By* in his club. But Ilsa persuades Sam, and he begins to play it.[16] Rick hears the song from across the club, and charges over to find out why Sam is breaking his rule. When he sees Ilsa by the piano, the action of the story rushes forward. The song affects the characters and the narrative and draws the audience into their world. All the painful memories come back, and they are forced to confront their past, present, and future. Similarly, *Falling Slowly* won the Academy Award for Best Original Song of 2007, appearing in the 2006 independent Irish film *Once*.[17] The main characters are musicians, and in a memorable scene they write the song together in a Dublin music shop. *Like As Time Goes By,* it affects them, moves the action forward, and draws us into their story.

It seems to me that God uses a similar technique. As far as we know, there is no divine soundtrack or voice-over to our lives. Perhaps God gives a running commentary to the angels about us, and an angelic orchestra plays sad, scary, or triumphant music over our daily scenes. If so, we do not hear it. God does, however, affect us and advance our stories with elements that occur within our world: Moses' sister Miriam sings about the horses and riders being swallowed by the sea,[18] David sings praises and laments, Mary lifts her voice in the *Magnificat*.[19]

This is why we never quite get a grip on God's plan; that is not the vantage point from which God speaks to us. We do not learn about life through some narrative voice-over from outside the world, nor do we hear the heavenly soundtrack hinting at what's about to happen. God speaks to us from within our lives, within our world, within our stories. The Author is not human, worldly, or the disembodied mind of the cosmos, but he has chosen to advance the action of this world's tale, and thus our lives, by words and songs on the tongues of other characters. We live in the pages, and he meets us on them.

What about prayer? Does the Author not speak to us from outside the story? Even in prayer—with rare exceptions—we do not hear a voice from outside of the story. It is the voice of the Holy Spirit, an actor himself on this stage, who whispers truth to us. Paul may have been given a vision of the third heaven,[20] but most of the time he says we get only glimpses and reflections.[21] John may have been given a revelation of the last and ultimate things, but even that occurred within the context of the story: an old man, exiled to the island of Patmos, is given a message for the Church, not a bird's eye view of history.

The playwright Arthur Miller said, "The structure of a play is always the story of how the birds came home to roost."[22] In other words, the story is a chain of consequences that arise from within the characters' choices. In our story, sin spreads like an epidemic across the ages from Adam and Eve, while redemption unfolds from Christ.

Every scene in our world, like the crying woman and the newspaper-reading man in the coffee shop this morning, fits into one of those two competing plot lines. Often it fits into both. Every moment moves us a little closer to life or death. And thereby hangs a tale.

- chapter 5 -

Things Fall Apart

"Things fall apart; the center cannot hold;
Mere anarchy is loosed upon the world."
—William Butler Yeats, *The Second Coming*

As I write this chapter, my coffee is getting cold. As I was writing yesterday afternoon, my pint went flat. The air pressure in my tires is down a bit, my house was cold when I got up this morning, my office keeps getting messy, and some money seems to have trickled out of my bank account since I checked the balance yesterday.

In 1850, German physicist Rudolph Clausius published a paper on what would become known as the Second Law of Thermodynamics. In 1865, he went on to develop it into the concept of *entropy*. Simply stated, entropy is the tendency for any system to become random or disorderly. In thermodynamics, it means that once you turn off the burner on your stove, the heat does not stay concentrated in your teakettle for very long. It dissipates into its surroundings (the air, the tea cozy, the trivet). In other words, it cools off. More generally, entropy is the tendency for any order to fall apart, unless energy is applied to keep it in place. When you stop pumping electricity into your freezer (during a power outage, for example), stuff starts to melt. Stop taking care of your lawn and weeds will grow. Stop cleaning your house and you will not be able to find your keys. Stop managing your business and it goes bankrupt. Dump a load of bricks off the back of a truck and they will not fall out in neat rows and stacks. The universe is not self-ordering.

In our cosmos, things fall apart.

But *why?* Why do we live in a universe where heat and energy dissipate, so that bright lights burn out, information gets garbled, and mountains eventually sink into the sea along with the decayed bodies of verdant plants and wonderful animals? The Law of Entropy explains *how* it happens, but not *why*.

Why? Well, because our cosmos is broken. Ah, and thereby hangs a tale...

The story begins in an orderly world, without human death. How do we know that? Adam and Eve are told that if they eat of the forbidden tree, they shall die. Paul tells us that death came through the disobedient choice of one man, Adam.[23] Humans, at least, were not designed to die. I do not know whether plants and animals died, and I admit that it is hard to imagine carnivorous animals in a deathless world. Was there entropy? Again, it is hard to imagine a universe in which hot things always stayed hot and cold things always stayed cold.

But something critical and essential in the cosmos snapped when Adam and Eve disobeyed God. The whole creation was "subjected to frustration," and put in "bondage to decay."[24] It seems absurd that the fate of all the heavens and earth should turn on this one scene. And yet, why not? As great armies might decide a war by a single combat, earth put forth its champion: a naked woman. Against her, a crafty serpent. With her, a naked, mute man. This contest would be to the death; no quarter would be asked or given. All was still, all was quiet. John Milton described what happened next in *Paradise Lost:*

> So saying, her rash hand in evil hour
> Forth reaching to the Fruit, she pluck'd, she eat:
> Earth felt the wound, and Nature from her seat
> Sighing through all her Works gave signs of woe,
> That all was lost.[25]

Some Christians affirm God's creation but argue that evolution was a process; he wielded evolution as an instrument to produce a good creation. If this is true, then apart from any other rational or scientific arguments I am troubled by this question: what exactly did we fall *from?* Is death not the operative mechanism of evolution? Is not death—often violent, lonesome death—the whole *point* of the evolutionary process whereby the strong survive and the weak are eliminated from the gene pool? Did the Spirit of God hover over the waves and say not "it is good," but rather that it is not good, and that the only way it would get better is for countless generations of lesser beings to starve, to freeze, to get eaten, to lose the race for survival? If God worked through the processes of evolution, then did God encourage misery and death to gradually achieve incrementally better creatures? Were millions of proto-Adams and proto-Eves forced to kill or be killed so that God could finally anoint one pair as "good," and give them a choice to obey? Or else. Or else what? Or else they would die, too, just as all their predecessors had? All of this is possible, and I cannot prove that it did not happen. Setting aside the details, that story does not have the same *shape* as the story in the Bible.

I am not a scientist, nor will I pretend that my viewpoint is based on empirical evidence. I do not believe that God created Adam and Eve without death and decay because of some fossil, but because of the cross and the empty tomb. The Gospel is about salvation, but salvation from *what?* Paul tells us that the last enemy to be destroyed will be death. Death is not God's friend, or his paintbrush, but his *enemy.* If we, as a race, were born into a world of death merely to thrash about and die again, with the world ending in the impact of an asteroid or the fizzling of our star, then what does our salvation consist of? What does Christ's resurrection save us from? What wrong does it right?

The story of Christ is about picking us up after a fall, and that implies that we have fallen from something that was worth the price of his life to restore. The whole logic of the Gospel is that we (and this world) were made for something better than this present state of affairs, and that while death entered the world through one man's disobedience, life has been restored through one man's courage and faithfulness. God-directed evolution is not a metaphor for this exchange, but a repudiation of it.

As Paul wrote in Corinthians, "If Christ has not been raised, your faith is futile; you are still in your sins. Then those also who have fallen asleep in Christ are lost. If only for this life we have hope in Christ, we are to be pitied more than all men...If the dead are not raised, 'Let us eat and drink, for tomorrow we die.'"[26]

We live in this story, traveling along its arc and carried by its momentum. We see death, decay, and disorder and try to understand it. Some of us believe that we have learned an ancient Story that explains the past and gives us hope for the future. There have been and remain other possible explanations. Some have speculated that perhaps only humanity is polluted, while outside our sphere of influence the creation remains pristine. The medieval astronomers imagined "the music of the spheres," as the planets danced through the halls of heaven, unstained by human sin. Today, some see humanity as a pollutant, a viral contagion infecting an otherwise healthy, natural world.

Others have shrugged off disorder and decay as the natural state of the universe, part of the random noise of the cosmos. In their view, any attempt to understand it, much less make sense of it, is doomed to fail. They counsel us to accept and embrace a life without ultimate meaning. William Shakespeare wrote these lines, spoken through the title character in *Macbeth,*

> Tomorrow and tomorrow and tomorrow,
> Creeps in this petty pace from day to day
> To the last syllable of recorded time,
> And all our yesterdays have lighted fools
> The way to dusty death. Out, out, brief candle!
> Life's but a walking shadow, a poor player
> That struts and frets his hour upon the stage
> And then is heard no more: it is a tale

Told by an idiot, full of sound and fury,
Signifying nothing .[27]

Many, maybe even most, of those who have lived on this planet have known in their heart that this is not the way it was supposed to be. We sense in our bones that we were made for more than this, that we *are* more than this. The majority report from the committee on the human experience is that we are more than just skin and bones, and death is not the end. Where does this impulse come from? Why do we feel so uncomfortable in our own skin? Would creatures produced by and adapted for their environment intuitively believe that they are misplaced within it? Do animals feel that way? Do fish rage against the ocean, or against their inevitable, long sink into its depths? Why do we? We have plenty of limitations that we do not question; we do not think it is unjust that we cannot breathe underwater, or that we cannot fly. Yet if illness or injury brings us unexpectedly to death's door, we feel that we have been wronged, that this cannot be the whole story of our existence. Why? What is the source of our sense of justice? Our attractions to sex or food or power are understandable, but where did our awareness of beauty and our sense of art come from?

Psychologists have explanations, but it is at least possible that we are rebelling and resisting because this is not all we are or were meant to be—or even all that we used to be. The Greek philosopher Plato suggested that there is some memory, buried deep in our bones, of how things were. Perhaps our DNA carries not only the congenital defect of the original sin, but also a racial memory[28] of better times and awareness of our true purpose. We were given this world to be our home, but we busted the place up and let it run down.

This dissonance is meant to remind us of the Big Story. Our frustration with life, our grief at loss, our toil to earn a living, our pain in childbearing: all of these are meant to draw us into the narrative. Pain and longing are a gift meant to prompt us to cry out, "Why are things this way?" Until we ask—no, until we shout—that question, we will never hear the Story.

The Christian Story tells us that the broken cosmos is a result of human rebellion. For some reason that has not yet been revealed, the Author made the condition of the universe dependent on humanity's relationship with God. This seems absurd, and I cannot imagine why it is so. That is the way stories are; there are connections and causalities and movements that only make sense later in the tale. Perhaps in some future chapter we will learn why a naked woman and her husband could break the cosmos, but at this point we only know that it is so. We have learned that the execution of a naked Palestinian Jew has begun to repair it. We also know that the whole creation is groaning like a woman in childbirth, longing to be freed from the shackles of decay. That will happen when we are restored to right relationship with God. We sift through the old stories and search the prophecies, trying to step far enough out of—or skip far enough ahead in—the story to grasp the mind of the Author, or at least the shape of the plot. This tale can only be learned as it is lived, one page at a time. Our cosmos is broken. It was not always so, nor will it always be. Its fate is tied to our own. But take heart: the third act has begun, and the Author has begun to turn the tale.

- chapter 6 -

About the Author

Most of us have never heard of Edward de Vere.

He was born in 1550, heir to one of England's most prestigious families. When Edward was twelve, his father died and he became the seventeenth Earl of Oxford and Lord High Chamberlain of England. He was a dashing and dangerous figure; at the age of seventeen, he accidentally killed a servant while practicing his swordplay. Both Oxford and Cambridge universities awarded him degrees in literature, and while such degrees were sometimes given to noblemen as a courtesy, Edward was said to be bright enough to have earned his legitimately. He became a leading member of Queen Elizabeth I's court, a poet, and a sportsman. De Vere was also a great patron, or financial sponsor, of many of the leading writers, musicians, and actors of the day. Dozens of books on religion, philosophy, medicine, and music were dedicated to him by many of England's leading intellectuals, who had received funding and encouragement from de Vere.

And some people think that he secretly wrote many of Shakespeare's plays and sonnets.

There have long been questions about whether William

Shakespeare wrote the works that bear his name. Some critics think that it is unlikely that a glove maker's son from an unremarkable village could have created a body of work with such nuance, mastery of form, and historical and cultural references. So, over the centuries, all sorts of theories have been floated about who might have written them under the pen name "William Shakespeare." One of the more intriguing suggestions is William de Vere.

The plays and sonnets exist, and so obviously someone wrote them. They are remarkable, and whoever did so was extraordinary. So scholars, students, and hobbyists listen to them carefully, trying to catch traces of a voice or stylistic ticks. They comb them for little hints of identity, and the subtle biases of a personality. They try to assemble clues to form a profile of the author. They work backward from what can be seen and known of the author's fingerprints, and try to match them with the known literary geniuses of Elizabethan England. Some think the evidence points to William de Vere.

In the same way, we feel compelled to ask: who is the Author of our stories? Who wrote the Big Story into which they are bound? Whoever it was, why did he write it, and who is the intended audience? In short, what can we learn from the creation about its Creator?

Some reject the notion that there is a creator. In the early twentieth century, the pioneering psychologist Sigmund Freud taught that we should free ourselves of the idea of God, with all of its constraints, guilt, and costs. Freud suggested that we had only invented God as a defense against the "oceanic feeling"[29] we feel as children when we realize that we are not connected to our parents and that the universe is vast. He argued that this sense of being adrift in the cosmic sea is terrifying, and our mind needs a safe harbor and a North Star to navigate us to it. Thus, Freud argued, we invent gods and religion as a coping mechanism.

For many, this is good news—even great news. Discovering that God is only a delusion can make one feel like a school child on the first day of summer vacation; suddenly, everything is possible and nothing is forbidden. Freud's "discovery" was part of a collective sigh of relief among the university intellectuals and café bohemians of Vienna and Paris around the turn of the twentieth century. One of them, Friedrich Nietzsche, described their exuberance as they ventured out into the cosmic sea without any admiral to obey, nor charts to follow:

> Indeed, at hearing the news that 'the old god is dead,' we philosophers and 'free spirits' feel illuminated by a new dawn; our heart overflows with gratitude, amazement, forebodings, expectation—finally the horizon seems clear again, even if not bright; finally our ships may set out again, set out to face any danger; every daring of the lover of knowledge is allowed again; the sea, our sea, lies open again; maybe there has never been such an 'open sea.'[30]

Nietzsche boldly declared that "God is dead" and that a new breed of man had evolved: a superman who was the captain of his own destiny and would bend the world to his own will. His ideas would profoundly influence a generation of young Germans developing a new sociopolitical movement. They called it the National Socialist Party, but we know them as the Nazis. Their leader, Adolf Hitler, enthusiastically embraced the liberation that Freud and Nietzsche described. Everything was possible, and nothing was forbidden.

Atheism is easy to suggest, but most humans have found it unsatisfying. Humans have never been able to free themselves from the idea, delusion or not, of gods or a God. The cosmos has the feel of something that has been *made*. A century or so before Freud and Nietzsche's confident assertions, the French philosopher Voltaire, who was as full of doubt and as skeptical of Christianity as anyone in his era, said, "If God did not exist, He would have to be invented. But all nature cries aloud that he does exist: that there is a supreme intelligence, an immense power, an admirable order, and everything teaches us our own dependence on it."[31]

At the beginning of the Modern Age, thinkers like Freud and Nietzsche boldly asserted our freedom in the cosmic sea. A hundred years later, postmodern secularism has found that isolationism unsustainable. In the last few decades, a surprising number of books and movies have suggested that our genesis on this planet is attributable to alien beings from other planets. The idea may have originated in science fiction, but it has become remarkably mainstream. Serious academics talk about a *pan spermia* theory of the origins of life. You may roll your eyes at the crazy notions of novelists, filmmakers, and college professors, but respectable society rolled its eyes at the Freuds and Neitzsches a century or so ago. If our academics and bohemians have rejected the Christian notion of God, they have felt it necessary to invent a new version. How badly does it speak of our need for a genesis story, a big narrative to make sense of our cosmos, that we replace God with *aliens?* How is that a better theory? I suppose that we get the best of both worlds: a Big Story narrative, but one that makes no demands on us for moral behavior. Aliens are our new Olympian gods, our new Valhalla. We get the benefits of a god-story without any of the nasty moral consequences.

No one thinks to ask how this does not just kick the can down the road. Where did the aliens come from? What narrative do they fit into? Or is it just turtles all the way down?

We try to make sense out of life in the cosmos by looking at the structure of the physical universe and drawing conclusions about its Creator. Paul said, "What may be known about God is plain...because God has made it plain...For since the creation of the world God's invisible qualities—his eternal power and divine nature—have been clearly seen, being understood from what has been made, so that men are without excuse."[32]

It is common to speculate on what the physical universe might teach us about its creator. Beyond the remarkable location in which our lives are set, we puzzle over the content of our stories. Why does life go the way it does? Why the bittersweet? Why are we saturated in joy at one instant, yet pierced with sorrow the next? Why do our hopes inspire us to race through life in pursuit of what we think we want, when what we need is so often just at hand?

Why do we need love so much yet abuse it so badly when we find it? If this life is just a valley of tears, why do we bother to hope at all?

Like the scholars who search the Shakespearean plays and sonnets, what can we learn about the Author from our stories? Who is he? What is he like?

One thing seems obvious: our Author apparently does not feel compelled to give our stories happy endings. We are generally willing to accept quite a bit of sadness in a story, if the ending is happy enough. Most stories work that way: the protagonist overcomes problems, even suffering, but emerges from them better off. So whenever we face troubles we keep waiting for the payoff, the twist, and the glorious finish that will have justified our pain. We tell each other that every cloud must have a silver lining, that it will all be worth it in the end, and that God has a plan to bless us—if only we will do our part to cooperate. Yet anyone who has been paying attention to the real world cannot fail to notice how many stories end unhappily. Sometimes bad lives end well, sometimes good lives end badly, and sometimes miserable lives end miserably. The ugly duckling does not always turn into a swan, slow and steady does not always win the race, the handsome prince does not always choose the girl with the heart of gold, and the oppressed often are not set free. The Author of our life stories does not always let us live happily ever after. At least, that is the way it seems from our vantage point within the stories. What does that tell us about him?

Here is another clue: our Author's story lines are long and complex. What are the boundaries of our stories, anyway? Where do they begin and end? A baby is born in some town. She grows up, she does this and that, such and such happens to her, she dies and is buried. When we think about her story, must we only consider those events that she experienced directly? Can her story to be understood to include the stories of her parents and ancestors, children and descendants? What about her village, her church, her nation, her race? If something in her grandmother's life had an effect two generations later, would that be part of her story? If her church contributed to a chain of events that affected a village half a world and half a century later, does that count as a part of her narrative? She might have never been aware of these longer, more complex plot lines moving through her life—but they did move through her, or she moved through them. We want our life stories to be self-contained episodes, but they are not. To pay attention to the world is to notice that our stories are rarely just our stories. To follow the narrative of our Author we must look at longer, more complex arcs of plot and character. What does that tell us about him?

Those two clues lead us to a third: the Author of our life stories does not seem overly concerned with justice in this world. People do not always get what they deserve in this life. There are causes and effects in this life, but rarely justice. Justice is a strange idea in a world with so little of it. If we are well evolved and adapted for life on this planet, then our insistence on justice seems misplaced. Our actual experience is that most of the time might beats right and that circumstances and accidents matter more than righteousness. We console ourselves with the notion that bad people will fail in the end. In the real world they sometimes do, but not always. As much as we wish it were not so, our ideals of justice do not always play out within our life spans. The clues seem to indicate that either the Author of our lives does not care about justice as much as we do, or that he does not always resolve our stories justly during our lifetimes. He is usually more concerned with grace, giving us what we need, not what we deserve. What does that tell us about him?

Here is another puzzling question about the Author of our stories: why does he write them in the first place? For whom? Who is the intended audience?

We are. He is telling us a story about himself, through us, and through each other. It seems like an unnecessarily complicated way to communicate with us. Would it not be easier to simply tell us what he wants us to know? Yet he is the great teller of true tales, and he wants us to pay attention and learn from them. Through the Big Story, through the Scriptures, and through the stories of other people, we learn the shape of the Author and the nature of his personality. Then we can, hopefully, read our own story as we live it and see the movements of the narratives into which we fit.

There is, I suspect, another audience as well. In the Bible, the book of Hebrews tells us that there is a great "cloud of witnesses,"[33] those who have come before us, who watch our lives and marvel at how their stories weave seamlessly into our own. They see the greater arc of the narrative, and they cheer and pray for us. I like to believe that they weep for us in our darker chapters, because they know what it is like to be lost in the pages. They rejoice in how the Author is pulling all the loose threads in this story together and in how he reveals himself in the process.

Beyond that, perhaps the audience is the cosmos itself. The very creation is watching, straining, and longing for our stories to be resolved.[34] How do we know what other sentient beings are paying attention? Angels, demons, and other characters we have not yet met might all be living within and following the Great Tale that the Author is telling. He hopes that through it all the cosmos will discover his true identity.

Part II

A Character's Life

- chapter 7 -

The Problem of Job

There once was a grasshopper that spent all summer hopping in the grass, singing songs. Meanwhile, his neighbor the ant spent the warm months dragging bits of food back to the anthill with his comrades, like ancient Egyptians hauling limestone blocks to a pyramid. When winter came, the carefree grasshopper found that he could not eat his summer songs. He looked longingly at the ants, living off the pantries hidden deep within their colony. He learned a bitter lesson when the ant lectured him about responsibility and preparation.

There once was a rabbit that was always bragging about how fast he could run. He liked to tease his neighbor the tortoise for being so slow. The tortoise got irritated, and challenged the rabbit to a race. The next morning they lined up, and the tortoise began trudging forward. The rabbit was unimpressed and bored. He decided to take a nap before starting. After his nap, the tortoise had only covered a third of the course, so the rabbit went to brunch. With a full meal in his belly, he fell asleep. By the time he woke up, it was too late: the tortoise was a yard from the finish line. The rabbit raced across the field, but even his speed was not enough, and the tortoise crossed the finish line first. As the rabbit lay there, panting and humiliated, the tortoise told him, "Slow and steady wins the race."

There once was a shepherd boy who got bored sitting in the field all day, watching the village sheep. To amuse himself, he shouted down the hill to the village, "Wolf! Wolf!" The men of the village grabbed their weapons and ran up the hill, only to find the boy laughing. They scolded him for wasting their time. He did not care, and the next time he got bored he did the same thing, with the same result. This went on for several days. Finally, he saw a real wolf prowling the edge of the meadow, eyeing the sheep. He shouted down to the village, "Wolf! Wolf!" This time, the villagers shook their heads and ignored him. When he did not bring the flock home that evening, they went up to the meadow, only to find the boy crying and the sheep lost and scattered. An old man seized the teachable moment and told him, "Nobody likes a liar, even when he's telling the truth."

Most of us like these kinds of stories; they make a quick point and illustrate some clear principle. What is more, the point is made directly to the characters before the end of their tale.

We have been conditioned by this type of story to expect events to teach us a lesson. Many of us expect life to be like one of Aesop's fables or Jesus' parables: whatever principles we are supposed to learn should be made clear to us within our life story. We are willing to accept conflicts, antagonists, and complications—as long as there is some point to it all. By the end of our lives, we want to be able to look back and understand how and why all the stuff that happened to us had to happen to achieve some purpose or to teach us some lesson. Life as a story? OK, but what is the moral of the story?

That brings us to the problem of Job.

Job is a book in the Bible, named for a man. He lived in the land of Uz, somewhere just south and east of modern Israel, in the country now known as Jordan. He does not appear to have been a Hebrew, but probably lived during the era of the patriarchs (Abraham, Isaac, and Jacob), sometime in the second millennium before Christ. He was what we might call a nomadic rancher and trader. The Bible tells us, "He owned seven thousand sheep, three thousand camels, five hundred yoke of oxen and five hundred donkeys, and had a large number of servants. He was the greatest man among all the peoples of the East."[35] Job was not just rich; he was also a good man. He "was blameless and upright; he feared God and shunned evil."[36] He obeyed God's ways. Like the Hebrew patriarchs, he served as a priest to his entourage. He offered sacrifices to atone for the sins of his family and sought to purify them from any unrighteousness. He enjoyed the fruits of this with a great home, beautiful wife, many children, good health, and a successful business.

Then, one day, everything went wrong.

A messenger came running up to Job to tell him that some enemies, the Sabeans, had attacked his oxen and donkey herds, carried them off, and killed Job's servants. While he was still speaking, another messenger ran up and said that, "The fire of God fell from the sky and burned up the sheep and the servants, and I am the only one who has escaped to tell you!" While that messenger was still speaking, another came up and breathlessly reported that, "The Chaldeans formed three raiding parties and swept down upon your camels and carried them off. They put the servants to the sword, and I am the only one who has escaped to tell you!" Before that messenger could finish, yet another arrived with even worse news. Job's sons and daughters had been feasting at the eldest son's house when a mighty wind swept in from the desert and blew it down, crushing all his children in the rubble. Job tore his robe and shaved his head.[37]

That was not Job's last bad day. Not long afterward, he was afflicted "with painful sores from the soles of his feet to the top his head. Then Job took a piece of broken pottery and scraped himself with it as he sat among the ashes."[38]

So, there was Job, sitting in the dirt. He did not curse God. Instead, he told his bitter wife, "Shall we accept good from God, and not trouble?"[39] He was willing to accept all of this—just as long as there was some good reason for it. He just wanted to know what that reason was. Why?

Three of his friends showed up. The book of Job is on the long side, and most of it consists of an extended argument he has with these neighbors about what ruined his life. Throughout most of the book they offer theories, and one by one Job bats them down. In chapter after chapter, Job tells them that he is certain that he has obeyed God's laws. Since God is not unjust or evil, he demands that God give him some explanation. He wants God to make sense out of why his life went down the tubes.

Job wanted his life to resemble the stories at the beginning of this chapter. He wanted to understand the relationship between his actions and what happened to him. He wanted to understand what purpose his life had accomplished. He wanted to learn whatever lesson his life was supposed to teach. He simply wanted to grasp the point of his suffering.

At the end of the book, God shows up. The Lord points out that it was he, not Job, who spoke the cosmos into being, who filled it with life, and who maintains it by his power and will. God makes it clear that he does not have to answer Job's questions. Job is told that he has no right to demand explanations for the events of life. God tells Job to worship, obey, trust, accept—and shut up.

Job is humbled by God's arrival and admonishment. He acknowledges that God's ways are far beyond his ability to comprehend. He accepts that whatever God does must—by definition—be right and fair. In a sort of epilogue, we read that God eventually rewarded Job's humility and restored his life. He was healed, got a new wife and kids, new cattle and servants. Then the story ends.

Many readers do not get it. God's answer to Job's questions is that Job has no business questioning him. God does not have to answer and so he does not. It makes most Christians uneasy. For all Job had been through, it seems rather insensitive on God's part. We assume that the story, including God's non-answer at the end, is supposed to teach us humility. We respect it because we have to, but it is not very satisfying.

Here is the problem: Job's story does have a point, and it does make sense. But Job never saw it, and God did not tell him about it. While Job is the central protagonist in his *own* story (as each of us are), he was only a minor character in a *bigger* story that he knew nothing about. The point of his suffering was not found within his tale itself, but in a larger and longer narrative. We know this because the book of Job shows the readers a few scenes from this other story. Characters that Job could not see or hear were doing and saying things in another place that directly affected his life. There was a bigger plot that he never grasped.

In the first chapter we read that Satan came to the divine council[40] after having roamed the earth. God told Satan to consider Job, who was blameless and upright. Satan said that Job only respected God because God had blessed Job with health and wealth, and that if that were to be taken away, Job would curse God to his face.[41] Satan insinuated that God buys people's love with goodies. He insulted the integrity of God's relationship with his followers. To prove Satan wrong, God twice unleashed the enemy onto Job. God intended Job's suffering to be an object lesson, making the point that his ways are not merely bribes.

Job's life was ruined, but he was not able to listen in on this heavenly debate. No one ever tells him that his sufferings are part of a wager being played out by God and Satan. The events of his life are simply elements in a longer story arc, a more complicated plot.

There are two morals that the reader is supposed to learn from the story in the book of Job. First, Job is told—

and does learn—that he must accept the wisdom and justice of God with humility. We are to understand that God's speech to him at the end could just as easily be directed at any of us. Who are we to question why God does what he does? God has purposes that we know nothing about, and he cannot and will not justify events within his kingdom (much less his actions in the larger cosmos) to us simply because we are caught up in them. Like Job, we must learn to trust that the Lord is good and rest in that trust.

The second lesson is for us, the readers of the book of Job, and not for Job himself. We learn that Satan cannot come between God and his people, no matter how hard he tries. Job is never taught that lesson, is never told the moral to his own story. Because Job could not read the first chapters of the book of Job (like we can) he never grasped the point of his sufferings, was never able to connect the events, and never got to see the lesson they teach.

Job was lost in the pages of his own story. He could not read the pages that he was not written on. His story only really makes sense inside a bigger story, and that one only really makes sense inside a bigger, longer story about the relationship between God, Satan, and humanity. These stories all only make sense inside the Biggest Story. Job's life makes perfect sense as a character in these narratives, and his sufferings are a necessary element in their structure. But only the readers (or listeners, or watchers) of these tales have a vantage point that lets them see what is going on.

Other cultures have accepted that we might be characters in larger stories, hidden from our vantage point. The ancient Greeks imagined their gods sitting on Mount Olympus, making capricious bets and embroiled in intrigues, with us mortals as pieces on their game boards. Even the Jews of Jesus' day believed that the source of our troubles was often found outside of what we do or see.

Jesus was asked about this problem. There was a man who had been born blind and spent all his days begging from passers by. The disciples asked Jesus, "Rabbi, who sinned, this man or his parents, that he was born blind?"[42]

The disciples were asking, *Why? Who did this?* Essentially, they puzzled over the same questions that Job asked, but about this poor beggar. What was the chain of events that led to this? Whose fault was it? What lesson was the blind man supposed to learn from his life? What principle does it illustrate? They wanted this man's life to unpack like one of *Aesop's Fables*. We do not know if this blind man ever asked these questions—Job's questions—about himself. It would have been understandable if he had.

Jesus' answer was in line with what we learned from reading the first chapter of the book of Job. He replied, "Neither this man nor his parents sinned." We are comfortable with Jesus dismissing the notion that the man's blindness was punishment for some sin of this man or his family. What should make us squirm is where Jesus does point the finger: your and my sin. This all happened so that Jesus could come along that day and give us all a reason to believe. The rabbi told his disciples, "This happened so that the works of God might be displayed in him."[43] Jesus seems to be saying that all the years that this poor man and his family suffered were a purposeful story. The events of his life—and the life of his family and those around them—would only make sense when they converged that day with two other plot lines: our unbelief and Jesus' life. This man was born blind so that you and I would have a reason to believe.

The Pharisees who objected to Jesus' healing of the man did not believe. Why not? We know in general terms: they were part of an entrenched and privileged leadership class, threatened by Jesus of Nazareth's challenges to their authority. That is one plot line in the biblical narrative, one arc in the bigger story. We do not know the hows and whys of the individual stories. Did this Pharisee choose not to believe, while another wanted to believe but could not, and a third secretly did, but was talked out of it by his colleagues? Were they, like Job, forever blind to the roles that they played as characters in a bigger story? Were they, like Job, lost in the pages?

We are all baffled by the injustices of life. Prosperity and poverty, happiness and sorrow, life and death—they do not seem to be distributed according to merit, or even righteousness. As Christians we believe that God is just and that somehow all will be made right in the end. That comforts us, but it does not answer our questions.

Even if we accept that God will make it all work out someday, we want to know why things happen the way they do today. Simply compensating us in heaven—like the maimed victims of some accident receiving payment from an insurance company—does not give meaning to our pain and suffering. Like Job, we are willing to bear a burden in service of some great purpose. We are willing to learn a lesson through our sufferings if God would only tell us what that lesson is. It is the nagging suspicion that our suffering is pointless that crushes our spirit.

This is the problem of Job: because our stories are caught up in even bigger stories, and because we do not get to read the pages that we are not written upon, our role in the Big Story is hidden from us. It is not mysterious in itself; like Job's story it might make perfect sense if only we knew what was really going on. As long as we are lost in the pages, much will remain a mystery, hidden before time began.[44]

- chapter 8 -

Life in the Present Tense

My father was an engineer, and when I was a kid he used to tell me that life was like building a bridge. Learn your math and grammar, and build your vocabulary. Learn life lessons from sports and part-time jobs. Talk to your school counselor and carefully plan your courses to line yourself up along a college-prep track. Each element is like a bridge pier, suspension tower, or girder. You look forward and plan, staging the various pieces so that the correct one is ready to snap into place at the correct time. Step-by-well-planned-step you will span the chasm of chaos that the unprepared and disorganized fall screaming into.

I love my dad, and appreciate the wisdom of what he taught me. I say similar things to my kids about their education. But the older I get, the less I think that life is a bridge-building exercise. It feels a lot more like a kayak trip.

Imagine that you are kayaking down a deep canyon, with a river zigzagging between steep walls. From your vantage point in the cockpit of your boat, the furthest that you can ever see is to the next sharp bend, never more than a quarter mile away. Every time you round a bend, the river presents a new situation that forces you to react. It might be full of house-sized boulders, with eddies and back-currents that you need to slalom through. It might be a torrent of whitewater, rushing down a chute or over a series of small waterfalls. There might be other kayakers on the river, competing with you to thread the obstacles. Hopefully, it will not be a really big waterfall. Now and then you might get a stretch of flat, slow-moving water where you can set down your paddle and rest while the current takes you along. Sometimes you find a beach that you can pull up onto and camp.

Obviously, preparation matters. This river will test your skills and equipment, and you cannot run it without the right training and tools. But after you have done everything that you can do to prepare yourself, you have to just take the river one bend at a time. You cannot plot or rehearse your moves in advance. Every few minutes you get a new set of challenges thrown at you, and you need to react to them in real time. You take the river as it comes.

Characters in a story take life one page at a time. Authors usually write in the past tense, but the characters live in the present tense. We want to forecast the trajectory of our story arcs so that we can anticipate how the plot lines of our lives will develop. In the first chapter of a novel, if we meet child with a passion for music and a gift for piano, we might assume that she will grow into a great performer, maybe even a great composer. That may be how bridges are built, but it is not how stories are told. We turn a page and the author makes us gasp with surprise: a vat of industrial acid explodes, melting away the gifted, young pianist's hands. How horrible! How senseless! How sad! And yet—this story just got interesting! What will happen now? We turn the pages as fast as we can read them, wanting to know how things will turn out for the crippled pianist. We get to the end and close the book, deeply affected by how the author wove the story threads together. But the poor pianist with disfigured hands can only live in the page that she is on. She takes the river as it comes, one bend at a time.

Life is like that, I think. We live in the present tense.

Then why do we not focus more on the present? We spend much, maybe even most, of our mental and emotional energy on two things that we have almost no control over: the past and the future. Obviously, we cannot control, change, or even mildly affect the past. The past has passed. Even so, behold how we obsess over it! Our yesterdays nibble away at our todays. We weep, regret, seethe, justify, and savor.

We have a little bit of control over our future, but not much. We can plan, prepare, and stack materials for our bridges. But there are endless possibilities that we can never anticipate. A tornado could destroy our towers, an economic crisis could steal our funding, or an epidemic could strike our workers down. For all we know, a prehistoric monster could rise from the chasm and knock our bridge down like a toy. We might find a malignant lump in our own body one morning, and the bridge might suddenly seem irrelevant. Of course we try to imagine the worst-case scenarios and design contingencies and redundancies. But as generals say, battle plans are only good until the first shot is fired. After that, we have to react and adapt on the fly. Once in the fray we have to live in the present tense. Yet we obsess over the future—what will happen, what might happen, what we worry about, what we hope for, what we want, and what we fear. Our tomorrows nibble away our todays.

Although we cannot change yesterday or control tomorrow, we can do something about today. We can decide what we will do right now. You can put this book down or keep reading. You can decide how you might live for the next five minutes, and how you might spend the next five hours. Each morning is like rounding a bend in the river. Maybe this is a whitewater day for you. You may need to paddle hard to the left, or shoot through a gap to the right, or pull over at a gravel beach. Maybe today is a smooth stretch, where you can put your paddle down and be carried by the current, taking in the scenery. You do not know what the next bend will bring, but that is out of your control anyway. If you want to be alive to see around the corner, then you need to concentrate on where you are. What will the next page in your story bring? The next chapter? Ten chapters from now? Who knows? This is the page you are on now. This is the page that matters.

Here is the key to living well: live well between now and the time you go to sleep tonight. When you get up tomorrow you will be on a new page. Do it again. If you keep doing that, the cumulative effect of all those well-lived days will be a life lived well. That is living in the present tense. Let us make no excuses about how yesterday has ruined today, or promises to live better tomorrow. Be good *now*.

This is how God wants his people to live. He wants us to concentrate on the page we are on, paying attention to what is happening now.

When the Lord brought Moses and the Israelites out of Egypt, he took them into the wasteland of the Sinai desert. There was no fruit to pluck, no roots or berries to gather, no fish to catch, no wild animals to hunt (at least not in enough quantity to feed the tens of thousands of Hebrews). So God provided. Every morning when they came out of their tents, they found dead quails lying on the ground. Apparently God caused flocks of these birds to fly overhead at night and then drop like stones into the camp. They also found some other stuff all over the ground. It was a flaky, white substance that could be gathered and smashed to form a kind of paste, and then cooked like some sort of grain cake over the fire. They did not know what to call this stuff, so they called it *manna,* which was Hebrew for, "What is it?" Every morning they went out and gathered a fresh basket of that "whatchamacallit stuff."[45]

There was only one catch: they could not gather more than a day's worth. If someone tried to gather enough to last for that day and the next, when they woke up the following morning it had rotted in the storage container. Every day they had to go out and gather that day's food, no more and no less. They had to trust God one day at a time. God wanted them to learn to live in the present tense.

After a number of months, the Israelites came to the bank of the Jordan River. God brought them there so that they could cross over into the Promised Land, which he had vowed he would deliver into their hands. Before they crossed, they sent a reconnaissance patrol over the river to check out this new country. Most of the spies came back with a disquieting report: the land was full of powerful people in well-defended cities. The invasion would be a disaster. They obsessed and agonized over what the future might hold.

Then they obsessed over the past, although their memory was selective. They ignored all the ways that God had provided for them, and instead rhapsodized about how good they had had it as slaves in Egypt. They gushed over how great the food had been and how much job security they had enjoyed making bricks for Pharaoh.

They had not learned the lesson of the manna. So God sent them back into the wilderness, for forty more years, until the generation that had disbelieved and doubted should pass away. That generation would never see the Promised Land. They had to wander until they died. Their children would be raised in the wilderness, eating their daily manna, learning to live in the present tense, one day—one page—at a time.

A few years ago some friends and I started a new Christian community. We called it Manna, because we did not know whether it was, or ever would be, a church in the usual sense of the word (remember, *manna* is Hebrew for "what is it?"). We were also at a moment in our lives when we felt that God wanted us to learn to live in the present tense. Not fixated on personal or denominational histories, nor too deeply invested in planning programs or growth.

Life in the Present Tense

We wanted to learn to live our stories one page at a time. Manna.

It has not been an easy lesson. The bridge-building metaphor was imprinted deeply into me. As a writer, I am always planning, working step-by-step on projects that take months or years to complete. I constantly fight the tendency to live my days in the future tense. Living in the present tense takes effort for me.

Because I find it so difficult to live in the present tense, I find myself constantly challenged by what Jesus said one day as a huge crowd gathered around him on a mountain:

> Do not worry about your life, what you will eat or drink; or about your body, what you will wear. Is not life more important than food, and the body more important than clothes? Look at the birds of the air; they do not sow or reap or store away in barns, and yet your heavenly Father feeds them. Are you not much more valuable than they? Who of you by worrying can add a single hour to his life? And why do you worry about clothes? See how the lilies of the field grow. They do not labor or spin. Yet I tell you that not even Solomon in all his splendor was dressed like one of these. If that is how God clothes the grass of the field, which is here today and tomorrow is thrown into the fire, will he not much more clothe you, O you of little faith? So do not worry, saying, 'What shall we eat?' or 'What shall we drink?' or 'What shall we wear?' For the pagans run after all these things, and your heavenly Father knows that you need them. But seek first his kingdom and his righteousness, and all these things will be given to you as well. Therefore do not worry about tomorrow, for tomorrow will worry about itself. Each day has enough trouble of its own.[46]

- chapter 9 -

Talking to the Author

Once upon a time there was a boy named Simon. Simon wanted—well, it is hard to say exactly what Simon wanted—but whatever it was, he wanted it badly.

Simon's father was a shepherd, and his mother was such a devout Christian that the Church later declared her a saint. When Simon was thirteen years old, he heard a sermon on the Beatitudes of Christ and began to fast and pray with the same zeal that other boys played sports or chased girls. By the time he was sixteen, he was living in a monastery. As a young monk, he fasted and prayed with such severe discipline that the other monks had to keep him from starving to death. He locked himself in a hut for over a year, praying and fasting for weeks at a time without human contact. But he wanted to get even closer to God, and so he eventually climbed a mountain and found a rocky height where he could be left alone to pray and fast. So many local people were impressed by his piety that they sought him out, asking for his prayers, blessing, or advice. The interruptions persuaded him that to get closer to God he needed to get further from the crowds.

Among the ruins of an ancient city in the desert, Simon

found an old pillar that was still upright. He climbed it and built a little platform to live on. People from a nearby village brought him food and water (not much, since he fasted so regularly). They put it into a basket, which he pulled up with a rope. Fifteen feet in the air, he was able to pray without distraction. The leaders of the Church in the region could not figure out whether it was a stunt to get attention or whether Simon was for real. After cross-examining him, they decided that he was sincere. People were so inspired by his passion for prayer that they built him a series of ever-higher pillars, allowing him to get closer to God and further from the world. Eventually, his pillar was more than fifty feet high, with a little platform just big enough for him to lie upon.

Simon's fame grew as the years went on. Christians came from all over the known world to watch and listen to him, and he felt called to devote some time each day to teaching them. They gathered below to listen to his sermons, and a few were allowed to climb a ladder to speak with him. Even bishops and emperors sought his advice. He wrote letters to his disciples and Church leaders as far away as France, sharing what he had learned in prayer. For Simon prayed, almost every hour of every day. He prayed in different postures: sometimes standing, sometimes kneeling, sometimes lying on his platform. Most of the time he would make a bowing motion while he prayed, bending his skeleton-like body over to touch his forehead to the wooden deck of his platform. One visitor, standing below, observed Simon repeat the motion 1,244 times before he lost count. It is hard to imagine anyone making a greater effort to live a life of prayer than Simon Stylites. He lived on his pillar for thirty-seven years before he died on it.[47]

He was no freak, no isolated phenomenon. We might think him so today, but for many centuries Christians aspired to get closer to God by retreating further from the world. Not everyone could afford to do that, of course. Most people raised families and crops, chopped wood, and caught fish. Those who prayed became heroes to those who worked, and they gladly supported their spiritual champions the way we support athletes and artists today.

Three hundred years later and a thousand miles to the West, other monks were so inspired by Simon Stylites that they built a community that would support his lifestyle. Instead of a fifty-foot pillar they found Skellig Michael, a seven-hundred foot rock spire jutting from the ocean twelve miles off the westernmost point of Europe—literally the edge of the known world. With North Atlantic gales whipping past and gulls circling below, they built a little monastery of stone huts, shaped like beehives, on a not-quite-flat ledge near the top of a nearly vertical mountain rising out of the sea.

The little community consisted of thirteen monks, to resemble Jesus and the twelve disciples. The villages on the coast probably sent out boats when conditions permitted (which was not often) to bring supplies. The monks were heroes to the average person, for they lived a life that most people could not live, but still greatly admired. What did the monks on Skellig Michael do through all those long days and endless nights? For the most part, they prayed. Seven times during every twenty-four hour cycle they huddled in the little stone hut that served as a chapel and said their prayers, rising in the middle of the night to stumble a few paces along their ledge through the dark, howling winds to talk to God together. When a monk would die, another would come from the coast to take his place. For nearly five hundred years this little house of prayer lived on the boundary between the known world and the mysterious ocean, between heaven and earth.[48]

Why? Why did Simon Stylites or the monks of Skellig Michael live this way? It offends our modern Christian sensibilities. To us it seems weird, a denial of what we consider the "real" Christian life. We ask, "What would Jesus do?" We are fairly sure that the answer is *not that.* If they wanted to get closer to God, we reason, why did they not they spend their lives sharing the Gospel with the lost, or serving the poor?

My point is not to defend the age of monasticism,[49] but to ask why they lived that way. The simple answer is that they wanted to speak with God more easily, more clearly, and more often. They considered dialogue with God to be worth living for completely.

If our lives are stories, what is the point of prayer? If God has already written our tale, why bother to ask for anything?

That very question reveals that we largely define prayer as *petition*—asking God for things. That says more about us than it does about God or the story that he has written. Real prayer goes far beyond petition. It is nothing less than a character's opportunity to speak with its Author.

It is remarkable that a creature, caught in a narrative, would get to dialogue with the Creator who is shaping the creature and spinning the tale.

Of course, the act of praying is itself part of the story. The character prays, God hears and responds.[50] The fact that God wrote the character's act of praying into the narrative is no different than the Author writing into the character the desire to pray (or the lack of desire), or the impulse to even consider it. We are creatures, and we will always depend on our Creator. Adam and Eve were seduced by a fantasy of independence, of becoming gods themselves. Prayer is no different from anything else: he made us, as well as our wants and actions.

Another medieval monk and saint, Thomas Aquinas, said, "We pray not that we may change the Divine disposition, but that we may impetrate [beseech] that which God has disposed to be fulfilled by our prayers."[51] In other words, our prayers do not persuade God to be generous or merciful; he already is. But when we pray we become worthy of receiving his generosity, mercy, and more. Prayer brings us closer to God so that we may receive, experience, and understand what he is doing in, for, and through us.

A child asks for what he or she wants, but a parent cares about what the child needs. As our Father, God cares about our needs more than we do. As the Author of our stories, he knows what is going on in chapters and plots which are out of our sight. He wants us to ask, but he also wants us to trust that he will bring our story to a joyful ending, whatever twists and turns we might take on our way there.

Jesus tells us that we should ask God for what we want

and that God will be generous and provide what we need. We should want more from him than just the satisfaction of our immediate needs, and that involves acquiring a taste for his Kingdom and character. As we want more *of* him, and less *from* him, our prayer becomes less about changing God and more about changing us.

Besides, why would we even want prayer to be principally about persuading God to change his mind or modify the story? What kind of relationship would we have with God if the only times that we talked to him was to ask him for things? What kind of human relationship would we have with someone that we only called when we wanted something? No doubt some of our petitions are kind and respectful. Others are flattering; some are angry, shrill, or whiny. That is not to say that we should not bring our needs and concerns to God. He wants us to ask him for things.[52] But when our prayers consist of nothing but petitioning God to do what seems best from our limited perspective, it is narcissism and arrogance, not worship.

Talking to the Author is ultimately about bringing ourselves into alignment with the story he is telling, not beseeching him to write it as we see fit. When we converse with him about it we engage in it, grasp it, and understand our role within it. When my friend is sick, I am living through a chapter my friend's story in which the Author has written that the sick person's friends ask God to heal and restore him. When I pray for my friend, I not only petition God for his health, I play my role within the story. If God makes my friend better, it is a story of answered prayer. If not, the story is of God responding in some other way. When we pray, we are like choir members singing the right line at the right moment in the cantata, or receivers running the right patterns in a football play. God is weaving our prayers, as much as anything else we do, into the Bigger Story.

Learning our role in prayer is harder today than it was during earlier centuries of the Church. We value individual feelings and the free sharing of them. Our prayers are full of what we feel, when we feel it, expressed in whatever form makes us most comfortable at the time. We chafe at the notion that prayer might be about feeling what we are supposed to feel, when we are supposed to feel it, and acting on that in ways we are supposed to act.

The pre-Christian Greek philosopher Plato thought that the purpose of education was to train us to think, feel, and act in ways that are appropriate to the situation, and for many long centuries Christians agreed.[53] Our education, particularly our religious education, was supposed to teach us how to respond as we lowered a friend into the grave, when we planted or harvested crops, as we confessed sin, or when we stood at the marriage altar. Rituals and liturgical prayers had the same function as sheet music for a choir and play books for a football team. Search for books with "Prayers for All Occasions" in the title and you will be astounded how many there are. The rules that governed the lives of medieval monks were scripts, and the players learned their lines.

The strategy was not foolproof. Too often, people just learned their lines and went through the motions. Their prayers became disconnected from their true feelings. They said all the right things, but their hearts were somewhere else. Familiarity bred contempt, and after a while the contempt for the ritual became contempt for the God they prayed to. Instead of moments of alignment and engagement with the Author, prayer and worship became hateful and hypocritical obligations.

That is one reason why Simon Stylites and the monks of Skellig Michael lived as they did. We have more technology, but the issues of the human heart have not changed a bit since their day. They knew that the gravity of this fallen world is always trying to pull us down with it. They knew that a life of prayer was in constant danger of becoming meaningless and ugly. So they sought to eliminate distractions and temptations. They arranged their lives to focus on conversation with the Author and to tune the rhythm of their hours so it drew them into the Story instead of dragging them away from it.

Today, Christians prefer prayers full of improvisation and free verse. We say whatever pops into our heads, and as a result much of our conversation with God consists of filler. We stall while we think of what to say next, and we repeat our favorite themes. Paul tells us that when we do not know what to pray for, we should let the Holy Spirit speak for us.[54] That is good advice; like an actor shouting, "Line!" when she has forgotten what to say, we are better off letting the Author speak through us than to keep babbling on when we run out of material. Of course, there are times when we need to pour our hearts out to God and ramble like an excited, happy, or terrified child. But if that is all that our prayers consist of, then we have not mastered the basics. Musicians, actors, and athletes can improvise after they have learned the fundamentals. The Church today does not teach us the fundamentals of how to talk to the Author. We make it up as we go along.

Jesus' disciples wanted to learn to pray, and so they asked him to teach them. Here is what he told them to say:

> Our Father in heaven, hallowed be your name, your kingdom come, your will be done, on earth as it is in heaven. Give us today our daily bread. And forgive us our debts, as we also have forgiven our debtors. And lead us not into temptation, but deliver us from the evil one.[55]

Notice how much of that prayer is asking God to bring us into alignment with his values and Story, not the other way around. It asks the Author to unfold his Story in history, and to make us a part of it. It does not ask for all our wants and needs to be met for the rest of our lives. It keeps us in the present tense by asking for today's bread, enough to sustain us on this page. And it asks for help in resisting the gravity of the fallen cosmos (our primary antagonist) and the harassment of the devil (an antagonistic character who makes aligning ourselves with the Story more difficult).

How odd was Jesus' prayer in the Garden of Gethsemane on the night of his arrest? Jesus knew the plot better than anyone; as the Author who has entered his own Story, he understood not only what must happen but why it had to happen and how it would end (that he would rise on the third day). It is understandable that his human nature did not want to go through the ordeal, and he presents a model for us of how to share our feelings with God. He also aligns himself with the Story: not my will, but yours be done.

So, what about Simon the Stylite and the monks of Skellig Michael? Were their efforts to talk to the Author misguided? Did their devotion bear no fruit?

How would we even begin to answer that question? Of all the prayers they said on their airy perches, who knows how many were answered? Of course that misses the point: measuring the value of prayer by the percentage of "successful" replies we get, as if we were evaluating a stock on its rate-of-return, is misguided at best. For the Christian, conversation with God is never a waste of time. Who knows what fruit it bore in their lives or the lives of others they prayed for? When measured by eternity, can we say that their prayers will not bear fruit in heaven? That is where we are supposed to be storing up fruit, anyway. Who are we to say that their lives on ledges were not the story the Author wrote for them, and a part of the Story? Can we say they were not an important part of it? Perhaps Simon and the monks on the Skellig were like obscure musical instruments that are only used during a brief passage of a symphony, or characters that appear only on one page of a novel. That does not make them unimportant, or unnecessary. We will have to wait until it is over to understand how they fit into the whole.

It is remarkable that we characters get to converse with the Author. Our prayers have been woven through our history: a prayer in a garden to remove a cup; through bitter tears as the cock crows for the third time; on the floor of the Coliseum as the lions come out the door; as the flames consume the martyr; as the soldier boy bleeds out and pleads for God and his mother; as the seeds are laid in the spring; as the thunderstorm tears the heads of wheat from the stalks; at the grain elevator as the harvest is sold and the money is paid; on the dock as the ship leaves and on the gangplank when it arrives; as the cold, dark waters pour through the torn bulkheads and fill the companionways; in the car in the parking lot before the job interview; in the doctor's office waiting for the test results; while staring at the bills and invoices; in the hospital; in the hospice; at the dinner table; during the worship service; before the committee meeting; in the locker room; by the bedside; before the test; before opening the letter; at the graduation; at the rally; at the graveside; after sharing the Good News and as the sinner accepts it.

In this Story, we talk to the Author.

- chapter 10 -

The MacGuffin

I like spy novels. When I need to shut out the world around me and entertain myself for a few hours—like when I am crammed into an airline seat—I love getting lost in a paperback full of intrigues and espionage. I read a good one on a flight a few months ago, and was trying to explain it to a friend later. The bad guy was a deep-cover agent, who had spent twenty years disguising his true identity. The bad-guy spy agency was desperate over some crisis and needed some secret information, so it activated the its agent and told him to do whatever was necessary to get it. The bad guy started bribing, stealing, and quietly assassinating his way through several European countries in pursuit of his mission. The good guy had to find out who was doing all of this and stop him. He chased him through the capitols and cafés of Europe, always just a step behind. I was telling my friend how absorbing the cat-and-mouse conflict was between these two characters that never discovered each other's identities until the very end.

The funny thing was that while I could remember the twists and turns of their interactions, there was an important detail that I could not recall. My friend asked me what the crisis was that precipitated the whole story. Why did the bad-guy spy agency activate the sleeper agent? What information was he trying to get his hands on? Why were the good guys trying to keep it under wraps? I sat there, racking my brain, and try as I might, I could not put it together. It was something about some decades-old secret agreement between Russia and Great Britain, and some files that exposed it. Or something like that.

Even weirder, the longer I thought about it, the less difference it seemed to make. The story was tightly written, the characters were complex, and the arc of how they pushed each other to change and grow was what really drew me in. The day of travel that I spent reading it went by quickly as I tore through the pages. Why they did things was less interesting than what they did, how they did it, and who they became in the process.

Sometimes an author needs a reason to get his characters moving. They are somewhere, doing something, stuck on some page. The author wants them to be somewhere else, doing something else. Maybe the author wants the characters to meet and interact somehow. He cannot just move them magically from one spot to another because then there would be no story (or it would be a lousy story). The author needs to give the characters some pretense, motivation, or circumstance that propels them forward through the narrative so that they can develop individually and together.

Fiction writers call this "the MacGuffin."[56] The MacGuffin could be anything. If it is a spy story, it could be a flash drive containing a secret chemical formula, and the characters chase it all over the world, trying to capture it for their government. If it is an adventure story, it could be a buried treasure that the characters search for through a jungle. If it is a legal thriller, it could be a closed case that gets reopened, forcing old witnesses to come out of hiding to testify. If it is a generational drama, it could be a grandfather's will that pits the children and grandchildren against each other, exposing the family's dirty secrets. The MacGuffin itself is not important; it is just a vehicle that drives the characters and action forward. If you think about it, you have seen or read a thousand stories like this. Six months later you cannot explain the details to a friend. You remember the hero, the villain, and what they said and did. Those are pressed into your mind. You do remember that they were trying to locate some file, or find a missing scientist, but exactly why starts to fade. It fades because it was irrelevant; the author's real intent was to show you his characters developing and interacting. That is what stuck in your mind. The MacGuffin was just the occasion that brought it about, and the details were not that important.

If our lives are stories told by God, then how many of the things that occupy us are just MacGuffins? What if the Author's purpose is to develop our characters and get us to interact with each other? Could it be that the details of the things we chase or build or react to are merely excuses to get us to grow and force us to cross each other's paths? Could it be that the *how* and *what* and *with whom* of our stories are more important than the *why*?

Broad swaths of humanity—not just Christians—have sensed that many of our plans and accomplishments in this life have little lasting value. Anyone who has strolled through a graveyard, or browsed through a used-book store, or wandered the ruins of some ancient fortress long crumbled and overgrown with weeds, has mused over the futility of the things into which we invest so much effort. We think that we are making our marks on the world, but very little of it survives beyond our lifetimes and egos.

The English poet Percy Bysshe Shelley described how foolish all our pomp and pretense will appear after it has been gnawed away by time. In his poem *Ozymandias*, he imagines a statue of Ramses the Great, Pharaoh of Egypt, rotting in the desert:

> I met a traveler from an antique land
> Who said: Two vast and trunkless legs of stone
> Stand in the desert...Near them, on the sand,
> Half sunk, a shattered visage lies, whose frown,
> And wrinkled lip, and sneer of cold command,
> Tell that its sculptor well those passions read
> Which yet survive, stamped on these lifeless things,
> The hand that mocked them, and the heart that fed:
> And on the pedestal these words appear:
> 'My name is Ozymandias, king of kings:
> Look on my works, ye Mighty, and despair!'
> Nothing beside remains. Round the decay
> Of that colossal wreck, boundless and bare
> The lone and level sands stretch far away.[57]

Perhaps the real value of the things we spend so much of our life doing is who we become in the process. The monuments do not last forever, but we do. Even monuments that do last might be less valuable than the act of creating them. I have had this thought while visiting some of the great cathedrals of Europe. Walk through Notre Dame, or Chartres, or York, or Canterbury. The architecture, the art, and the sheer scale of the devotion to God humbles the soul even after seven or eight hundred years. Yet I cannot help but to wonder: did God need this? Is his majesty enhanced by this magnificence? Is Christ any more exalted by this beautiful pile of stone? Certainly it is of great worth that generations of believers have been inspired by these places and pointed toward God.

The stories of how these cathedrals were built might be a hint of their ultimate purpose. Many of them took a century or more to complete. That meant that the artisans who conceived of and designed them did not live to see them finished—and they probably knew that when they began. For perhaps a hundred years, the lives of entire families were wrapped up in building a cathedral. Villages became towns and then cities around it. Generations of citizens contributed money. Generations of farmers, woodcutters, and quarrymen supplied materials. Generations of cooks fed the workers. Craftsmen taught their sons the secrets of their trade. Children were conceived, born, baptized, raised, apprenticed, married, and then had their own children who buried their parents in the shadows of the slowly-growing walls.

In the end, what really mattered for eternity: the cathedral, as beautiful as it is, or the act of building it? Could the cathedral have been a MacGuffin in the hands of the Author? Could its real purpose have been to weave generations of little stories together? When I go out of my way on a trip to visit one of these places, is it a MacGuffin that bends my plot and winds my thread into the old, old cord of all those lives?

I have been involved in a few church building programs over the years. The rhetoric soars when the vision for a new church is cast; the advancement of the Gospel and the growth of the Kingdom seems to hang on whether this structure goes up. I know that churches need buildings, and great things can happen inside and through church buildings. But if Notre Dame Cathedral could be a MacGuffin, then how much more could a church building in Atlanta or San Diego or Bogatá be simply an excuse for God to get us up, moving, and doing his work?

How many MacGuffins does the Author drop into our individual life stories? How many of the things which we chase and fret about are not really important, other than to give us a reason to work, love, meet, talk, learn, travel, build, and give? I cannot remember what gifts I gave or got for most of the last twenty Christmases, but I remember shopping, I remember the kids coming downstairs in their pajamas, I remember our family going through our weird little traditions on those mornings, I remember friends coming over for dinner on those afternoons. For all the worry about what to buy or ask for, the gifts do not even seem worth remembering compared to the love we shared or the memories we made around the tree.

Not everything we pursue is a MacGuffin, of course. There are plenty of things that we do in life that really do matter. Certainly, going into all nations, making disciples, and teaching them to obey everything the Master has taught us is no mere plot device.[58] But from time to time, the Author tosses us MacGuffins to move our stories forward. He uses them to put us in places and with people where the things that really matter can happen. While we chase our MacGuffins, God sends the real adventures. As John Lennon said, "Life is what happens while you're busy making other plans." Do what you have to do. But when you are someday standing in heaven, sharing the wonders of your story with a friend, do not be surprised if you cannot remember all the things that seemed so important at the time.

- chapter 11 -

The Desires of Your Heart

Why does God break our hearts?

It is inevitable that some hearts will get broken in a broken world. We might agree that for some hearts to get changed, God needs to break their hard, outer shells. As they say, to make an omelet you've got to break some eggs.

But some hearts get broken in a way that seems unnecessarily cruel, and hard to reconcile with a God who loves us.

On a trip to San Francisco a few years ago, an acquaintance asked me why God made homosexuals. We were eating downtown by the waterfront after a meeting. He remarked that since we were in a city with such a famous gay community, he had a question that he had always wanted to ask a Christian. I was not sure if he was going to ridicule my faith or if he was really curious, but I told him to ask away. He said he believed that homosexual desires were innate, that some people's brains were just wired to be attracted to the same gender. Since God had made them this way, he asked, how could God then tell them that the natural object of their sexual desires was off-limits? Why should they not be able to fall in love, get married, and experience complete lives? Why would God force them to choose between obedience and human fulfillment? Were they doomed to heartache? He grinned, as if he had trapped me with a contradiction in my faith.

Whatever his motives in asking, it was an excellent question, and I told him so. I pointed out to him that homosexuals are not the only ones who struggle with wanting things that they never will, or maybe never should, have. Most of us would like to be richer or skinnier, for example. Some of us want things that, if we got them, would be physically or morally harmful. These are the normal frustrations of life, and most of us are mature enough to realize that we cannot have everything we want.

Yet for some of us, the heartache is fundamental to our identity. Some of us are made in such a way that we can never feel complete, never fulfill our most basic instincts and character impulses, because something is forever kept just beyond our reach: the childless woman, the paralyzed athlete, the lusty eunuch. Why would the Author make holes in us that can never be filled? Why give some hearts desires that can only break them? Why give us love without the possibility of a beloved, or thirst that cannot be quenched, or itches that we are forbidden to scratch? Why would the Author create characters that can never be happy?

Most of us are willing to accept the consequences of faith; we will fight for what is right, and hope that we would be strong enough to withstand persecution or even martyrdom if it were ever necessary. The cost of discipleship seems worth paying when great issues are at stake. But why should some of us be condemned to being forever sad? Is the Kingdom of God advanced, or the powers of darkness in this world challenged, when some of us go through life frustrated and miserable?

Does this sort of frustration risk driving us away from him, into bitterness? Many of the people I meet who have actively chosen to reject the Gospel do so because of a broken heart, not an intellectual investigation of the claims of Christ. Most of those do not even realize this about themselves. They have rationalizations and justifications for their position, but talk to them long enough and you can hear the hurt seep from their souls. Somewhere, somehow, they were deeply disappointed by life, and they do not trust God. I have known genuine intellectuals that used reason and study to protect them from a God they believe has let them down. As the comedian George Carlin once said, "Scratch a cynic and you'll find a disappointed idealist." Is this a risk that God took in creating the human soul? To be able to love, did we need to be made capable of heartbreak and of lashing out when love turns sour?

Perhaps God wants some of us to have a holy discontent with this world. Perhaps the Author knows that these folks would settle for the thing that they want so badly, and never look past it to him, its source. Heartbreak reminds us that this world is not enough. God takes a risk with pain, hoping that it will drive us to him. In the fifth century, Saint Augustine wrote, "Thou hast formed us for Thyself, and our hearts are restless till they find rest in Thee."[59] We are far too easily pleased by this world. We were made for so much more. Perhaps, in his wisdom, the Author wrote some of our stories as restless searches, hoping we would eventually discover joy.

If God satisfied all our hungers in this life, would it spoil our appetite for the feast in heaven? This raises an interesting question: can we be "bought off" with rewards in the afterlife? In his excellent book *Christ the Tiger*,[60] Thomas Howard argues that no amount of Valhallas or Happy Hunting Grounds really make up for the hurts of this world. It is not good enough, he says, for God to hand us a harp and a robe and tell us to forget about the rape and the cancer. Howard says that instead of buying us off, Christ redeems the heartbreaks of this world; he takes them, transforms them, and gives them back to us, not as happiness, but as joy. Joy is more than happiness or even contentment. Joy is a deep blessing, an ordination of all that we are and all we have been through, and it is only given birth through pain and labor.[61]

There is a Bible verse that I have heard many times on the lips of the disappointed. They cling to it as if it were the deed to their dreams. They pray to redeem its promise. This verse of exceeding hope tells us to, "Take delight in the LORD, and he will give you the desires of your heart."[62]

This verse is easily proven false by observation. How can God promise to give us the desires of our heart when so many of us clearly do not, will not, and indeed cannot get them?

Perhaps we need to re-calibrate our desires.

If you are like me, you became immediately suspicious when you read the previous sentence. Whenever I hear something like that, I suspect that I am about to get swindled, asked to settle for less, to adjust my expectations downward. I figure that someone is smiling as they run the old bait-and-switch game. Good news: the job description/ product/hotel room/sale price/rental car/government program that you were lured in with is being substituted with something even "better" (or they swear that you will eventually realize that it is better). But I do not want a God who bait-and-switches me, who promises me the desires of my heart only to tell me that since I desire the wrong things I need to learn to smile as a lesser substitute is slid in front of me. Many have turned their backs on God because that is exactly how their Christian experience went. They heard the Gospel; it relieved their fears, ignited their hopes, and fueled their imaginations. Then they discovered the Christian life. They had to settle for the Church as it is, not as they dreamed it would be. They found themselves being asked by Christian leaders to accept too many disappointments in life. Over time, they felt ripped off and tired of making do with less. They wanted their son back, their body healed, their debts (financial, not just spiritual) canceled, their careers to be rewarding (financially and spiritually), their spouse to be a better person, and so forth. Their pastor told them they were supposed to be content. They tried, they really did. But deep down inside, they were not. They wished that the preacher telling them to be content did not sound so—preachy. They longed for more and were afraid to say it for fear of sounding ungrateful.

But what if our desires themselves are merely settling? In other words, what if we desire too little, not too much?

I knew a woman I will call Grace. She taught me something profound, something about the deeper themes of the Big Story and how to think about our little stories within it. She never explained it, she just illustrated it, and through Grace, by grace alone, I grasped it. I have not learned to do it yet, but I am trying.

Grace's husband was a drunk, with everything that came with it. He could not hold a job, he mishandled their finances, and he lied to her. He even physically abused her. Of course she desired love and a husband who would be trustworthy, kind, and devoted to her needs. As her pastor, I would have understood if she had divorced him, turned her back, and shaken the dust off of her feet. I could not have looked her in the eye and asked her to settle for this louse when she longed for so much more.

Grace saw it differently. What she taught me is that there are three possibilities for how to resolve the conflict in the third acts of our stories: the *merely good,* the *harder better,* and the *awful best.*

Our most basic option is to do what God requires, no more and no less. We can be minimal Christ-followers: sincerely accept the Gospel, worship, belong, and serve. We can do our best, with the Holy Spirit's help, to obey his commandments and repent sincerely when we fail. We can participate in and be grateful for the sacraments. When a spouse is unfaithful or abusive, it is within our rights to separate or even divorce. There is nothing wrong with that, and no one will hold us at fault. This is the *merely good.*

Jesus told us to do some rather hard things, as did the

apostles. When someone slaps us, we are to turn the other cheek. We should not worry about what we shall wear or eat, for God clothes the flowers and feeds the birds. When we give, we should hold nothing back. Living up to these standards takes not only more faith and endurance, but also different expectations of God and life. It means we count our rewards in heaven, not on earth. This is the *harder better*.

There is another way: holiness. Now, all of Christ's followers are sanctified (set apart for God), and since Christ extends his righteousness to them, we are all made holy on his account. Beyond that, we can become personally holy. We can take on God's character in such a way and to such a degree that Christ is represented and reproduced in our actions. We can reflect Heaven's light and become a beacon in a world of dark and stormy nights. Our stories can become almost sacramental, with grace spreading to others through us.

Think about what it would mean if our feelings, choices, and actions became truly Christ-like. Jesus died with other men's spit in his beard. Being holy is life-laying-down love. True holiness is appalling, almost offensive in its rejection of every normal human instinct and every worldly value. The holiness of Jesus does not win admirers; it is considered foolishness by this world. "He was despised and rejected by mankind, a man of suffering, and familiar with pain. Like one from whom people hide their faces he was despised, and we held him in low esteem."[63]

This is the *awful best*. I call it awful because it fills me with awe—it is itself a thing full of awe and wonder. Of all the forms that the third act of our little stories can take, holiness is the most glorious. Through holiness, the divine shreds our talk of desires and rights. I balk at the idea of asking, much less demanding, that someone else make the awful, best choice of personal holiness. I do not think anyone can achieve the awful best by trying to "do" it, anyway. Holiness is not something that you do, but something that you become. You only become holy when you truly want what God wants, truly love what he loves, and truly strive for what he strives for. When your plot line becomes his plot line, you find him. When your heart desires what his heart desires, then he will satisfy the desires of your heart.

Grace became my parable of the awful best. She separated from her husband, for the drink made him do bad things. She tried to get him treatment, with limited results. But she never divorced him, even though she could have. That would have been the merely good, or even the harder better. For more than thirty years, she went over to his apartment several times a week to help prepare meals, do laundry, shop for and put away groceries, balance his checkbook. Other people, including many good women in the church, thought that Grace was nuts. They had labels for her: *enabler, codependent, doormat.* Many people said that she was not doing him, or herself, or anyone else, any good. She had a right to live her own life and a right to her own hopes and dreams.

Grace was small, silver-haired, and seventy-something. When asked about her commitment to her husband, she had a simple answer. She remembered standing before God and promising to serve him for better and for worse. Because her husband had not done the same did not let her off the hook. In her eyes, her marriage vows were not a contract with the groom, but a covenant made with the Lord. Jesus loved her husband and had died serving him. She had committed to do the same. She wanted to see as Jesus saw, love as Jesus loved, and serve as Jesus served. Her attitude and actions offended almost every value we hold as a culture. Her desires had been transformed. As to her rights, she had laid them down. She had become like one from whom people hide their faces, and many people esteemed her not.

Why does God allow our hearts to break with unmet longings? I do not know. I suspect that our stories could not have joy unless they contained heartache. I do know this: if by our third act we can grow his heart in our chests, it will be unbreakable.

- chapter 12 -

Generations

How long does it take to tell a story?

Well, it depends on the story. For example:

This morning, I drove downtown to meet a friend for coffee. The end.

I know, that's not much of a story. To be a story, it needs conflict, a problem to be overcome, and some resolution. Let's try again:

This morning, I drove downtown to meet a friend for coffee. It snowed hard last night, and the plows hadn't been out. I was slipping and sliding all over the road. I saw several cars stuck in ditches or smashed into trees. Even worse, I realized that I didn't have enough gas to get there. I stopped to fill up, but my debit card wouldn't work at the pump. I had a hard time believing that, since I'd checked the account balance online before I left the house. Frustrated, I had to walk across the street to a cash machine. It was treacherous, trying to cross the boulevard through slush and ice while dodging traffic. Fortunately, it must have been something wrong with the card reader at the gas pump, because the machine spat money at me. I had to cross the street again, through the slush and the cold, blowing wind. A passing truck splashed through a deep puddle of grimy slush, ruining my pants. I paid the attendant, then wondered if I was going to get hypothermia standing by the car while filling up with wet, slushy pants (my wife would have waited in the car while it pumped, but I'm too proud and not as clever). Anyway, I was fifteen minutes late by the time I got to the coffee shop. My friend had assumed I had stood him up, and had already left. I called him on his cell to apologize. Fortunately, he was only down the block and came back to meet me. A couple of cups and some conversation later, I'd almost forgotten about my frustrating journey.

More like a story, huh? It's still weak, and too ordinary; the underlying conflict (whether I'll make my meeting in time) is merely circumstantial—all I had to do was endure some inconveniences. There was no real antagonist. There was no character arc: I did not change through the story, and the story did not change me. It is the kind of story that, if I told you about it on the phone, you would be bored and probably doing something else while you listened, hoping I would finish up quickly.

The story would have more depth if it forced me to make some hard choices and do some difficult things to overcome conflict. It would be more engaging if I evolved through the narrative in reaction to events. It would be more interesting if we learned more about my friend and his story. It would have been more interesting if some really unusual things would have happened: if my bank account had been cleaned out by Russian hackers; if I had slid into the ditch in a blizzard and been forced to survive on the old, stale French fries under the seats in my car; if my friend had been kidnapped by aliens and I had rescued him. If all of those had happened I might consider negotiating for the movie rights to the story.

Here's a more intriguing question: when did my story begin? This morning when I woke up? Last week when I set up the meeting with my friend? Two years ago when I met him? Fifteen years ago when I moved to this town? And when does the story end? When do the events of this morning conclude?

Generally, we think of a narrative as a series of connected events. We follow the chain of connection back until the causality (one thing causing another thing to happen) peters out. That is the beginning of the story. We reach the end when the chain of causality fades to black. My little story above is contained within a morning's time.

But our stories are somehow all connected; it is stories all the way up, and all the way down. One moves us into the next. There are also very long stories that cannot be completed in one lifetime, because the chain of causation goes back many generations, and the plot takes many more generations to develop. Sometimes the story is not about any one character, but a multigenerational epic that none of the generations can grasp while in the midst of it.

God likes these generation-spanning stories. The Bible focuses more on multigenerational epics than individuals, tracing arcs through nations, races, and families. Promises are made to one person, but kept hundreds (or thousands) of years later, and hundreds (or thousands) of miles away.

The tenth chapter of Genesis is sometimes called "The Table of the Nations." It is the sort of thing that gets skipped in preaching and devotional reading, which is too bad, because it is an important clue to understanding how

God works in our world. It begins by telling us, "This is the account of Shem, Ham and Japheth, Noah's sons, who themselves had sons after the flood." It describes the family tree, through several generations. Noah's sons Japheth and Ham produce descendants that are infamous in Biblical history. For example, from Noah's grandson Javen (through Japheth) come "Elishah, Tarshish, the Kittites and the Rodanites. (From these the maritime peoples spread out into their territories by their clans within their nations, each with its own language.)"[64] Verse six tells us that the sons of Ham were Cush, Egypt, Put, and Canaan. Cush was the father of Nimrod, a mighty hunter (and war-like man?) from whom, Genesis 10 tells us, the Babylonians and Ninevites in Assyria were descended. We read that Noah's grandson Canaan was the source of the Canaanite tribes and the nations, territories, and languages that would figure so prominently in the story of Israel. The chapter teaches us that the Israelites themselves trace their origins back to Noah's son Shem.

This family tree frames the narrative that comes after. The various nations are often spoken of as if they were a person, with the name of the most significant ancestor. One generation unleashes a chain of events that affects the culture of its nation for centuries. The character, choices, and conflicts of ancestors play out in the lives of the nations they sire. New lives are not blank canvases, waiting to be filled by individual choices. The canvas is shaped, and partially completed, by those who came before. Each generation can add only a limited amount of material, within the boundaries that were given to it. When it is our chapter, our turn to step onto the stage, the tale has momentum and inertia. We can only affect its trajectory, not set it.

The Author shows his bias for this approach in the most unlikely of places: the Ten Commandments. The second commandment forbids the people to make and worship idols of false gods. God then tacks on an ominous comment:

> I, the Lord your God, am a jealous God, punishing the children for the sin of the parents to the third and fourth generation of those who hate me, but showing love to a thousand generations of those who love me and keep my commandments.[65]

This is harsh to the ears of a culture that prizes individualism: it seems unfair to punish me for something that my great-grandfather did. But is that not the way the world actually works? Do our choices not cascade downward through the generations? One brother immigrates to another continent, finding a new vocation and maybe even converting to a new religion. The other brother stays behind and holds to the old ways. Fifty or five hundred years later their descendants have little in common but DNA. Civilizations are rarely built or torn down in a single lifetime. On those rare occasions when they are, the forces which crested in the pivotal generation were set in motion long before.

So when God says that he "punishes the sins of the fathers to the third fourth generation of those who hate me," at the very least he is warning us that the consequences of idol-worship are far-reaching. God does more than simply *allow* our choices to affect our children. He says here, and other places, that sometimes he actively shapes our lives based on our ancestors' choices. We are born in original sin, we commit personal sins, and we inherit generational sins.

Lest we become discouraged about the legacies that we get and give, let us pay attention to the second half of God's explanation. He promises to punish the children for the sins of the parents to the third and fourth generation of those who hate him "while showing love to a thousand generations of those who love me and keep my commandments."[66] The contrast is intentional, and important. Generational blessings far exceed generational curses, at a ratio of 1,000:4. In fact, if we understand the "thousand" to be a figure of speech meaning "to the maximum" or "infinitely," then God's comment on generational stories takes on a very different meaning. In his mercy, God limits the consequences of our bad choices in the lives of our descendants, blessing them *as much as possible*. Thank God that he punishes our families, churches, tribes, and nations only to the third and fourth generation for our sins; then there is still hope for us. The Author tells long tales, but they contain far more grace than pain.

The story of God's people began with his promises to Abram of Ur: he would become the father of many nations, he would inherit the land, and his children would be as numerous as the stars of the sky or the grains of sand on the beach.[67] But Abram never saw any of those things. He had only two sons, and one of them was driven into exile (where he would become the father of nations whose stories would keep crossing paths with the story of his half-brother's people, down through the generations to today).[68] Abram (later renamed Abraham) died without seeing any of this happen.

The promise was not forgotten. More than a thousand years later, Abraham's descendants wondered whether they were still a part of Abraham's story. In reply, God sent them this message:

> Can a mother forget the baby at her breast and have no compassion on the child she has borne?
> Though she may forget, I will not forget you!
> See, I have engraved you on the palms of my hands; your walls are ever before me.
> Your children hasten back, and those who laid you waste depart from you.[69]

Although it is sometimes hard to understand our role in stories that started long before we were born (and will not end until long after our exit from the stage), the chapter into which we are born still matters. We carry the seed for the next generation, passing on the learning and the legacy, the wealth of the generations, to our children. The genealogies of Jesus are full of people who were not famous, but through their blood and faithfulness the line of David was passed on. In the fullness of time a savior was born in David's town. Some of us get to live in chapters where the story turns dramatically, and our role is active.

For example, Queen Esther was the wife of the king of Persia. God placed her in the heart of Persian luxury and power, but she was of Jewish descent. The ancient story of Abraham ran in her veins. When a plot to exterminate the Jews was uncovered, her uncle urged her to use her proximity to the king to rescue her people. The queen was reluctant to risk herself for Israel's descendants. Her uncle reminded her that the story was bigger than she was:

> Do not think that because you are in the king's house you alone of all the Jews will escape. For if you remain silent at this time, relief and deliverance for the Jews will arise from another place, but you and your father's family will perish. And who knows but that you have come to your royal position for such a time as this?[70]

Should we not see our own lives in the same way? Some things that happen to us only make sense in the context of our great-grandparents, or in what our great-grandchildren will experience.

It is common to worry that we have not accomplished enough in, or with, our lives. This anxiety usually takes one of two forms.

Some of us feel that we have not left enough of a mark on the world. We were not famous, or famous enough. We did not rise high enough above the crowd to be remembered a hundred or a thousand years from now. Our family name will not be carried on. Throughout the ages people have aspired to this kind of immortality. Trying to live forever on the pages of history, they have fought wars, built kingdoms, created works of art, and strove for political office. Philanthropists have endowed hospitals, universities, and libraries so that their names will be repeated over and over, long after they can no longer hear. But fame is a cold and fickle goddess who cannot be easily bought. Many must roll in their graves today, realizing that they have been forgotten by the world that went on without them.

Some of us have another worry: that we have left too much undone. We passionately care about something: people who have not heard the Gospel, the poor, medicines not yet invented, injustices not yet corrected, threats not subdued. It feels irresponsible for us to leave so much undone in this world.

When King David died, the Kingdom of Israel was not everything that it could or should have been. The Promised Land had been subdued, and the borders of Israel were as wide as they would ever be. Despite these blessings, the nation's faith in Yahweh and commitment to the covenant was a mile wide and an inch deep. Just below the surface were disbelief, disunity, and discord. David had conquered, but not converted, the nation. It was a projection of his own heart; he had loved the Lord deeply but not consistently. He had served the Lord but just as often had served himself. He united the twelve tribes but could not unite his own household. The enemies of Israel had been driven across her borders, but they waited for the opportunity to attack again. The pagan idols had been pulled down and put away but not destroyed or discredited. The Ark of the Covenant, the Lord's house, was still in a tent. God had forbid David to build him a permanent temple. The name of the Lord, and the peace and justice and goodness that it should have brought, had not yet been taken to the nations.

Most of us will never achieve as much as David did, but we can relate to the sense that too much of what we should accomplish is incomplete. That is when we must remember that the Lord works through the generations. Each of us is only a chapter in a long story. It is not our part or place to get everything done. The most that we can do—and the most that God will hold us responsible for—is to accomplish his purposes in our time and place. The Author assigns us a role and we live it out. How could we ask for more? How could we do more? If our chapter was a productive chapter, then it was a good chapter. We should not be ambitious for fame. Instead, we desire that what was said about King David would be said about us:

> When David had served God's purpose in his own generation, he fell asleep; he was buried with his ancestors and his body decayed.[71]

If we accomplish the Author's purposes for our generation, for our chapter, for our time and place, then we should be able to die content and go to meet the Lord. When we do, we should long to hear this:

> Well done, good and faithful servant! You have been faithful with a few things; I will put you in charge of many things. Come and share your master's happiness![72]

Really, what more could we want?

Part III

Irreparably, Irrevocably, Irrecoverably, Irremediably

- chapter 13 -

Is It Written?

The 1962 Academy Award for Best Picture, along with six Oscars, went to *Lawrence of Arabia*. The film was based on the true story of T.E. Lawrence, a British military officer during World War I who helped organize an Arab insurgency against the Ottoman Turkish Empire in the Middle East between 1916 and 1918.

At one point in the film, Lawrence devises a plan to lead a force of fifty Bedouins across the Nefud Desert to make a surprise attack on Aqaba, an Ottoman fortress on the Red Sea. The native Bedouins consider it madness to attempt a crossing of the Nefud, a vast plain of sand dunes without a sliver of shade or a drop of water to be found. Lawrence persuades them to try, and they travel at night, hiding beneath makeshift tents during the day so as not to exhaust themselves or their camels. Several days later, they reach the other side and approach an oasis in the shade of some cliffs, just as the sun is rising. Then they notice that one of their comrades is missing, his camel trudging along without a rider. They assume that the man, Gasim, must have fallen asleep during the night and dropped from his saddle. Lawrence insists that they turn around, or at least send a search party back to find Gasim. With the sun rising and the Nefud heating up, the more experienced Bedouins tell Lawrence that venturing back for a search would be suicidal. They tell him that, from their Muslim perspective, it must have been "written" that Gasim would fall and die that night. To attempt to rescue him, they argue, would be to contradict Allah's will.

Lawrence will hear none of this. While they go on to the oasis, he turns around and heads back into the sand. He finds Gasim, barely alive, and brings him back to the others at the oasis. The Muslims are impressed. Lawrence then uses the incident to drive a point home to their leader, who has been skeptical of him. "Nothing is written," says Lawrence.

This is, of course, heavy with irony: the entire incident, including the line, "Nothing is written," *was* written, by the screenwriter. It was written into the script that the other characters would believe that Gasim's fate was "written," and that this would make perfect sense to them. It was also written into the script that Lawrence would believe that Gasim's fate was *not* written, and that this would make perfect sense to him. It was written into the script that Lawrence would rescue Gasim based on his belief that the man's fate was up to him, while his companions went on, believing that it was not. It is confusing, but in this story the characters ponder, believe, choose, and act on both well-considered motives and wild hunches—but the story came from a screenwriter fifty years later, sitting outside of the real-life Arabia. Whether he based it on real events or imagined the whole thing, Lawrence's character really does (within the world of the story) choose to take the risk and rescue the man. Inside the world of the story, the choices and actions were real and free.

This brings us to the doctrine of predestination.[73] Some Christians believe it to be a Calvinistic distortion of Christian theology, reducing us to mere puppets jerked around by divine wires. Predestination raises an awkward question: is it written? Is the story already set? Are we just actors forced to perform a script? If so, why even bother to speak of motives, choices, justice, or even love?

The truth is (as is often the case) more complicated than that. John Calvin did not cook up the notion of predestination in the sixteenth century. Calvinists did emphasize it, but since ancient times it has occurred to many people—not just Christians—that fate, destiny, gods, or even the planets[74] might influence or even control our lives.

Ancient Greek mythology tells of three women, the *moirae* (meaning the "apportioners"), called the Fates in English. Clad in white robes, they apportioned life to humans. Clotho spun the thread of life from her distaff onto a spindle, and Lachesis measured the thread given to each person. Atropos chose the manner of each mortal's death, and at the appropriate point cut their life-thread with her Shears of Destiny. The idea of the Fates seems to have been buried deep in the ancient Eurasian consciousness; Norse mythology also has goddesses called the *norns* who played a similar role, as did the Baltic goddess Laima and her two sisters.

Greek mythology is our best-recorded sample of the ancient Eurasian worldview, and beyond the Fates it largely viewed humans as the pawns of divine forces. *The Iliad* and *The Odyssey* are not just tales of a bad war and an even worse trip home from it. Those plots are merely the stages on which the real plot plays out: how the gods affect and determine the lives of men, usually for capricious reasons. The plots of the great stage plays of classical Greece usually featured a character trying to avoid a fate that chased him relentlessly; no matter which way he ran he was unable to escape its grasp. In Sophocles' *Oedipus Rex*, the chorus just offstage haunts and taunts the protagonist until he discovers the story that has been written for him. As the chorus chants, Oedipus realizes that his doom has been written.

Others have approached the problem from a more philosophical or even mathematical approach. Aristotle suggested that the universe was a vast machine, events always caused by prior events. Follow the chain of causality in the cosmos back to the beginning, said Aristotle, and you must get to a *prime mover,* something like a person with a billiard cue who initiates the game by breaking the cluster of balls set on the table. Some have toyed with the idea of *determinism,* going so far as to imagine that if you could know the exact position, speed, and direction of travel of every particle of matter in the universe—and you had enough computing power to crunch the numbers—you could predict the future in the same way that you could build a computer model to predict where all the billiard balls will go when they are struck.

Astrology is a profoundly deterministic worldview, in

which the planets control human events (including our thoughts, feelings, actions and choices), and these mechanisms can be known and predicted. Interestingly, in recent decades the mumbo-jumbo of traditional astrology has been given a more scientific facelift, with all sorts of charts, calculators, and so forth. These are supposed to make us more confident that the astrologers are simply analyzing the predictable movements of the cosmos, which supposedly control us as surely as the three Fates of ancient Greece with their spinning wheel.

Even though we suspect that the game of life might be rigged, we still want to be free to make our own choices and set our own course. We do not want to just read lines and follow stage directions from a divine script. We want to improvise. When it comes time for divine rewards—whether they are health, happiness, heaven, or hell—it seems unfair to award them based on thoughts or actions that were out of our control. The whole idea plays havoc with how Christians usually think about the Gospel. Did God not punish Adam and Eve for making a bad choice? How could he do that if they were not free to choose? Are we not promised eternal life if we confess that we believe in Christ? Why does God bother if he puts the words into our mouths? Do Christians that believe in predestination tend to become the "frozen chosen:" complacent and not bothering to share the Gospel since God will pick whomever he chooses, regardless of what we do?

Christians have tried to reconcile predestination with free will, floating various possible solutions to the problem.

One is to simply embrace determinism: accept the fact that God controls everyone and everything. As I write this, he is making my cat choose to paw the screen door to be let in or out for the fifth time in the last hour. He is making me choose to become angry at the cat and frustrated because I must either stop writing and get up, or listen to her paw and whine. And—here we go—God has written into my story that I've chosen to get up and let her in. Hold on, I'll be back in minute...

Another approach to the problem is to downgrade God's control of us to merely foreknowledge. God is all knowing, right? So if God knows everything, then he must know what will happen in the future, right?[75] So he does not make me get up and let the cat back out (after I let her in seven minutes ago!), he just knows (and always has) that I will let her in and then right back out. This approach tries to soften predestination: God does not *make* our choices, he just *foresees* them. This does not really solve the problem, because God is not just all-knowing, he is also all-powerful. If God knew in advance how irritating my cat would be this afternoon, why did he go ahead and make the world this way? Could he not have given me a less annoying cat? Or no cat? Or more resistance to her pawing?

It is bad enough with our pets, but what about evil? If God knew that the man down the road would sexually abuse his daughter, or that Hitler would send Jews to the concentration camps, or that the tsunami would drown thousands of people, why did he go ahead and allow those things to happen? Does that make God responsible for them? If God knew that my friend would reject Christ, and went ahead and made him that way anyway, then how can God fairly punish him for that by sending him to Hell?

Philosophers who deal with this problem would call the premise of this book a type of "compatibilism." Calling God the divine Author of stories that we live out might be a wise solution, or it might be the coward's way out of the problem. It certainly is the easy way out; this book argues that God's will and our free choices are compatible. I am convinced that both scripture and reason teach us that God somehow determines all the events of the cosmos, including my choices. Does he merely anticipate and allow them, or does he proactively bring them about? Both and neither, I think. He has written a Big Story which contains billions of little stories. We are the characters in them, and he brings that story to life. That is, I think, compatible with moral responsibility. In this story my cat is neurotic, and her neurosis makes her want to go in and out the screen door every ten minutes. In this story I am weak and easily distracted by the cat, I cannot stand to listen to her paw the door and whine, and I keep using that as an excuse to stop writing. That is what happens inside this story, and the fact that it was written by an Author does not make the characters any less responsible for their choices or actions.

Our frustration with predestination and our insistence on free will spring from a hazy notion that we should somehow be able to stand outside of the story and evaluate it, as if we were actors who had been told to perform a script that we thought was poorly written. If an actor wanted to change what his character says or does, he might get angry when the director tells him to stick to the script as written or else he'll be out of a job. He might feel constrained by the lousy script, angry that he is being forced to say and do things he objects to on stage. He can hold that opinion because the actors are not the characters; the actors live in the real world outside of the script.

We cannot really step out of the cosmos, can we? To where would we step? What vantage point do we have outside of ourselves? If I am unhappy with my life or world, is not my discontent part of my story? If I do not like who I am or what is going on around me, it is because God has written that discontent into my character at this point.

What the Bedouins in *Lawrence of Arabia* were feeling that morning was "fatalism." They reasoned that there was no point in going to rescue Gasim, because it seemed clear from circumstances that Allah had already written the ending of Gasim's story. They did not think it through far enough. Fatalists assume that if events are headed in a certain direction, and if the probability of a certain outcome is high enough, then challenging that outcome is pointless. Why should we think that? In the case of Gasim in the Nefud desert, the script was written in such a way that Lawrence would be there, and would choose to risk himself to rescue Gasim. There may have been a low probability of success from where they were standing, but it was the twist in the story. The story included a long shot that went into the goal. A fatalist gives up trying to affect the plot, never realizing that our choices and efforts are themselves part of the story. Who knows what might happen if we try? The only way to find out is to make the effort and turn the page.

There is a story about an ancient con man that served a

king as the court magician. For some reason, he fell out of favor with the monarch. The king ordered his head to be chopped off, and the guards stepped forward to frog-march him from the throne room. As they grabbed him, he called out, "Wait, your highness! What if I could teach your cat to sing and dance?"

The king raised his hand and the guards stopped. "Could you really do such a thing?"

"Absolutely," said the magician. "And with a dancing, singing cat, you would become the richest, most famous king in the whole world!"

"This is true," said the king, daydreaming while petting the cat on his lap. "How long would it take?"

"One year," said the magician.

"Very well!" the King pronounced. "I will give you one year, locked in the tower with Fluffy. If on this day, twelve months from now, Fluffy cannot entertain the court, then your head will be on a stick outside the walls as a warning to others not to lie to me."

Fluffy was handed to the magician, and they were marched to the tower. As they climbed the stairs, one of the guards, who was friendly to the magician, asked him if he was crazy. "Do you really think you can pull this off?"

"Probably not," shrugged the magician. "But a lot can happen in a year. The king might die. The cat might die. I might die—or escape. And who knows, the cat just might learn to sing and dance. We'll have to see what happens."

Believing that the Author has written our story does not stop us from believing, choosing, or acting within it. We are fearfully and wonderfully made, and so are our personalities and circumstances. We have no idea how our characters are going to develop and what the consequences of our choices will be. We could only know those things if we could step outside of the pages and read ahead in the book—but we are lost in the pages. We live and love, choose and act. As the story unfolds, we discover what we are becoming.

- chapter 14 -

Cracked Pots

Some books have a problematic chapter, one that makes both author and reader uncomfortable. Everyone is tempted to skip it. This is that chapter. I put off writing it as long as I could. It gives me no pleasure to reflect on this topic. If you are flipping through the book, you might be tempted to keep flipping, but I hope that you do not. As much as we would both like to, we cannot avoid talking about Hell.

Here is the dilemma, as plain as I can say it: not all of our little stories will have happy endings. Some fraction of them (I have no idea how many, nor do you) will end grimly. This seems inevitable in any story with good guys and bad guys: the woodcutter rescues Little Red Riding Hood and chops off the wolf's head, the wicked witch melts, Gollum clutches the ring and falls into the fires of Mount Doom. Not only does it resolve the plot, it brings justice to the story.

Can there be any doubt that there are bad guys in our stories? Simple observation tells us that there are: the serial killer who kidnaps and tortures children, the con man who swindles little old ladies out of their life savings, the genocidal despot who uses rape and famine to steal from the poor and advance his megalomania, the abusive priest who plunders a child's innocence, the depraved emperor who tied Christians to poles and burned them alive to illuminate his garden parties. These and so many, many more are characters in our plots, and in the Big Plot.

In our bones, most of us know that evil demands a reckoning. We grasp that unless there is some justice in the narrative of the cosmos, then it is just space full of random and mostly ugly events. As Christians, we know that we are supposed to love the sinner and hate only the sin. We remember that Jesus told us to turn the other cheek—but when we think about the monster who corrupts children we feel better remembering that Jesus also said, "If anyone causes one of these little ones—those who believe in me—to stumble, it would better for them to have a large millstone hung around their neck and to be drowned in the depths of the sea."[76]

Of course not all bad guys come to bad endings. Many antagonists change in the third act; even Darth Vader turned into a nice guy in the end. Sometimes, what appears to be a villain may only be so from the vantage point of one of our particular little stories: a British Spitfire dogfights with a German Messerschmitt over London in 1940—one pilot will be the villain to the other's children. Sometimes one character causes others to suffer during his darkest chapter, but his story becomes redemptive in the end (in *Les Miserables,* Jean Valjean steals a loaf of bread, which was no doubt hard on the owner of the loaf, but it saved

Valjean's starving sister and her family—and in the end he redeemed himself by protecting Cosette). It is possible that we live in a story in which every character eventually turns good before the last page. That is a hopeful and generous way to look at our story; perhaps Christ redeems all characters in the end by reconciling all things to himself.[77] Sadly, I do not think that is the case.

The Bible never describes Hell. There is no systematic, theological discussion of the subject. There are no details about where it is, what it is like, or how it works. God unfolds reality and teaches us what we need to know through stories. This is especially true of Hell. Perhaps it is such a grave subject that God knows we can only grasp it through story and imagination. Jesus taught us about Hell by weaving it through many of his parables. In fact, Hell is the whole point of some of them. Consider the following examples.

Once upon a time, there was a rich man who sat around all day gnawing on turkey legs like Henry VIII in an old Hollywood movie. All the while, a poor man begged outside his door. The rich man would not even toss the beggar a dinner roll. They both died. The poor man went to heaven with the saints of old ("the bosom of Abraham"). The rich man went to a place of fiery torment, where he was in agony. There was a great chasm between the two places, which no one from either side could get across.[78]

Once upon a time, there was a king who held a wedding banquet for his son. He butchered his fattened cattle, decorated the hall, and otherwise prepared a first-rate party. He sent his servants to tell the guests that everything was ready. One-by-one they made lame excuses for not showing up. They beat and killed the servants that brought the invitations. They insulted and rebelled against the king, and disrespected the son. Angry, the king ordered his servants to fill the hall with anyone they could find; to go to the street corners and round up passersby so that the feast he had laid out could be enjoyed. When the party was in full swing, the king came into the hall and found a man who had not taken the time to clean himself up and put on wedding clothes. He had shown no gratitude for the favor that had been given to him. Angry, "the king told the attendants, 'Tie him hand and foot, and throw him outside, into the darkness, where there will be weeping and gnashing of teeth.'"[79]

Once upon a time, there was a landowner who built a vineyard, and rented it out to some tenants. When the harvest came he sent his servants to collect the rent. They beat, stoned, and killed the servants as they arrived. Exasperated, he sent his son, figuring that the tenants would at least respect his heir. When they saw the son, they murdered him, hoping to steal his inheritance. The owner eventually came, and brought those wicked tenants to a wretched end.[80]

Once upon a time, a landowner had his fig tree cut down and burned because it consistently failed to bear any fruit.[81]

Almost as much as love, Hell is a consistent theme, whether overt or implied, throughout Jesus' teaching.

If your hand causes you to stumble, cut it off. It is better for you to enter life maimed than with two hands to go into hell, where the fire never goes out. And if your foot causes you to stumble, cut it off. It is better for you to enter life crippled than to have two feet and be thrown into hell. And if your eye causes you to stumble, pluck it out. It is better for you to enter the kingdom of God with one eye than to have two eyes and be thrown into hell, where:
"the worms that eat them do not die,
and the fire is not quenched."
Everyone will be salted with fire.[82]

Any talk about the destruction of the wicked is jarring to our modern ears. Yet there it is, right on the pages of Scripture next to passages promising blessings and rewards. When Jesus met two demon-possessed men, living among some tombs on the edge of town, they screamed at him, "Have you come here to torture us before the appointed time?"[83] Peter explains that if God did not spare angels when they sinned, but sent them to "hell"[84] to be held for judgment, "Then the Lord knows how to rescue the godly from trials and to hold the unrighteous for punishment on the Day of Judgment."[85] It is intellectually dishonest (not to mention spiritually presumptuous) to deconstruct that sentence and pay attention only to the promise to rescue the godly. Hell is integrally woven throughout the New Testament. The Gospel is only good news because of the bad news that lurks in the background.

Clearly, our Story has villains and some of them will meet rough justice. That raises uncomfortable questions: if God is the Author of this Story, is it fair that some people are cast as the villains? How is Hell fair, when those who go there were only playing the parts written for them? If God writes their stories, could he not have written an ending without Hell?

To wrap our minds around this we have to start here: God chooses to do this because he *can*. Whether we think of God as a divine novelist, sculptor, or builder, he has the power and prerogative to create as he sees fit. To us it may seem arbitrary and capricious for God to assert his right to cast some creatures as villains and then turn around and punish them for their villainy. Sometimes we act as if we are the first generation to have discovered this monstrosity in the Bible. We tell ourselves that this doctrine was the product of an intellectually primitive or morally insensitive age, and that it must never have occurred to the biblical writers that this doctrine is offensive. Of course that is not true: the apostle Paul knew very well that this doctrine offended first-century Romans. In his letter to them he plunged into the heart of the matter:

> What then shall we say? Is God unjust? Not at all! For he says to Moses, "I will have mercy on whom I have mercy, and I will have compassion on whom I have compassion." It does not, therefore, depend on man's desire or effort, but on God's mercy.[86]

The Author will cast his characters as he sees fit to tell the Story he wants to tell. We do not choose our parts in the divine drama. Paul continues:

> For the Scripture says to Pharaoh: "I raised you up for this very purpose, that I might display my power in you and that my name might be proclaimed in all the earth." Therefore

> God has mercy on whom he wants to have mercy, and he hardens whom he wants to harden.[87]

The reference to Pharaoh teaches us something about how God unrolls our Story. In the book of Exodus, God sends Moses to tell Pharaoh to allow the Hebrews (who were enslaved building Egyptian monuments) to make a three-day journey into the desert for a worship festival.[88] He gave Pharaoh incentives: a series of devastating plagues and natural disasters that would cease only if Pharaoh would relent. At points during the negotiations, Pharaoh wavers, wondering if keeping the Hebrews is worth the cost of devastating his nation. Whenever Pharaoh seems tempted to give in, God stiffens his resistance ("hardens his heart"). The Lord not only cast Pharaoh in the villain's role, but at moments in the narrative when Pharaoh could have taken a different course, God wrote his character in such a way that he did not. Like a tragic play from ancient Greece, in which the chorus keeps warning the character to turn aside and avoid disaster, Pharaoh is driven to his doom. Paul argues that the whole point of Pharaoh's character is to be the villain, so that the plot can unfold and the Lord can rescue the Israelites from their plight. Through that story, we are to learn something about the Author.

This does not just sound unfair to our ears; it sounded unfair to Roman ears two thousand years ago. Paul anticipates their reaction:

> One of you will say to me: "Then why does God still blame us? For who resists his will?" But who are you, O man, to talk back to God? Shall what is formed say to him who formed it, 'Why did you make me like this?' Does not the

potter have the right to make out of the same lump of clay some pottery for noble purposes and some for common use?[89]

Paul argues that we start to understand this only when we accept that God can cast characters (or make his creatures) however he sees fit. An author can conceive of any sort of world he wishes, lay out the locations, cast its characters, set their motives, construct the plot lines, and organize the chapters. In this Story—our Story—some characters are protagonists and some are antagonists. Some evolve and change. Some arcs are surprisingly redemptive, and some are darkly tragic. As Paul says, just as the same lump of clay can be divided and made into both the good china and the dog's food bowl, so God will reveal, over the course of this Story, each character's purpose. Paul writes,

> What if God, choosing to show his wrath and make his power known, bore with great patience the objects of his wrath—prepared for destruction? What if he did this to make the riches of his glory known to the objects of his mercy, whom he prepared in advance for glory.[90]

Now we come to the heart of the matter, the reason the Author wrote villains into this Story: because it "makes the riches of his glory known to the objects of his mercy." In simpler terms, that means: *so that the protagonists would be able to understand the Story, and in understanding the Story come to understand its Author.* As the plot turns, redemption unfolds. Some characters are carried through the danger and pain of this broken cosmos by the mercy and love of the hero (the Author who has entered his own

Story). They suffer under relentless villains who will not let them go. While lost in the pages of their lives, they discover grace in instances of love and episodes of mercy. They see some hearts harden and some soften, and they learn that the choices that soften a heart are gifts, not accomplishments. They hear the tale of the hero, of the Author-made-character who promises a never-ending story to those believe it, and they follow him. They cry out that they want to believe—but that too is a gift. Looking backward, they see their story arcs drawn together inside the bigger story arc, and they find in that grace the God they could have come to truly know no other way.

What about the villains whose hearts God never softens? Yes, God has the right to write his story however he sees fit. Yes, those characters that receive grace can appreciate the gift by contrast with those who do not. Yes, the villains deserve justice (just as we do, but for the gift of grace). Was there no other way? If God could have given grace to all, should not he have done so? Is Hell necessary?

As odd as it sounds, perhaps Hell is an instrument of God's mercy.

Our Story contains bad choices, rebellion, and misery. Once those elements infest the cosmos, what is to keep them from virally spreading, metastasizing, corroding the universe from the inside out? Where can those story arcs end?

Perhaps, in his mercy, God made Hell to contain and limit suffering. Perhaps he said, "This is misery's boundary. Beyond it the cosmos will be free of stain. Life will be abundant, and my banquet will be joyful."

God has decreed that evil cannot veto good. Spite will not be allowed to dampen the creation's joy. If there were no Hell, the wicked would have a place at the banquet, and God will not allow his joyful celebration to be spoiled by those who will not celebrate. Rebellion against God's sovereignty serves a purpose in the Story, but it will not be allowed to ruin the ending.

I have come to believe this is true. I cannot say that it makes me happy. I trust the Lord when he tells me that there is a day coming when there will be no more crying or pain.[91] I trust that on that day, Hell will not spoil my joy, it will secure it.

The seventeenth-century English poet and preacher John Donne wrote about the awe, dread, and surrender that come when we acknowledge that we are merely characters from the Author's pen. In one of his most famous meditations,[92] Donne confessed that he turned to God for peace in a world that seems to beat us all down. Then, Donne says, he found, "That all the wounds I have, come from thy [God's] hand, all the arrows that stick in me, from thy quiver." We might take comfort, Donne says, if God gave only blessings, because then we could blame the difficulties of life on other sources. But when Donne grasps that the Author is the ultimate source of all the conflicts and confusion in his story, he is forced to acknowledge that

mine enemy is not an imaginary enemy, fortune, nor a transitory enemy, malice in great persons, but a real, and an irresistible, and an inexorable, and an everlasting enemy, The Lord of Hosts himself, The Almighty God himself. The

Almighty God himself only knows the weight of this afflic-
tion, and except he put in that *pondus gloria,* that exceeding
weight of an eternal glory, with his own hand, into the
other scale, we are weighed down, we are swallowed up,
irreparably, irrevocably, irrecoverably, irremediably.[93]

We are lost in the pages, but not hopelessly so.

- chapter 15 -

The Antagonist

In too many stories, the devil gets all the good lines.

Take *Paradise Lost,* for example. John Milton knew how to write a villain like no one else. His 1667 epic poem describes the fall of Lucifer from Heaven, and Adam and Eve from Eden. Milton's Satan is an awesome creature. The greatest of the archangels, the poem begins with him and his army of rebellious angels picking themselves up off of Hell's floor, to which they have been tossed from Heaven's heights. In the poem, Lucifer is portrayed as a noble being, powerful and heroic. When he learned that God intended to create Adam and Eve and to endow them as his children, his pride spawned jealousy. Twisted by ambition, he turned his considerable gifts toward thwarting God's purpose in creating humanity. From the depths to which he has been cast, he launches a daring plan: he will tempt God's new favorites to revolt, just as he has done. He will spite God by vandalizing his creation.

So Milton has Satan deliver epic lines, like the following:

> To reign is worth ambition, though in Hell:
> Better to reign in Hell than to serve in Heaven.[94]

and,

A mind not be changed by place or time. The mind is its own place, and in itself can make a Heaven of Hell, a Hell of Heaven.[95]

and,

So farewell hope, and with hope farewell fear, Farewell remorse: all good to me is lost; Evil, be thou my good.[96]

Over and over again in literature, the antagonist is more interesting than the protagonist: Milton's Satan, Goethe's Mephistopheles, the monster in Mary Shelley's *Frankenstein,* Tolkien's Gollum, *Star Wars'* Darth Vader, even *The Silence of the Lambs'* Hannibal Lector. Authors often rely on a strong antagonist to focus the protagonist's struggle. A strong antagonist makes the story clearer for everyone: the hero, the author, and the reader.

This raises an obvious and awkward question: who is the antagonist in our Story?

Satan? That is the first thing that comes to mind for most Christians. The Bible has passages that would certainly make us think so. For example:

Put on the full armor of God, so that you can take your stand against the devil's schemes. For our struggle is not against flesh and blood, but against the rulers, against the authorities, against the powers of this dark world and against the spiritual forces of evil in the heavenly realms.[97]

It has always been tempting (pun intended) to think of

Satan as the opposite of God, or at least as the opposite of Christ. That sort of *yin* versus *yang* symmetry is an appealing way to frame our worldview, not to mention the conflict in our Story. But Satan is not God's equal. He is not even Jesus' equal. He is not even in their league: he is a creature, the same as you and me. He is vastly more intelligent and powerful than we are, but the Father, Son, and Holy Spirit created him just as they created the blue whale swimming in the Pacific and the ants under your feet. The Bible infers that he led an angelic rebellion in heaven against God, and that he was cast from Heaven with a third of the angels—but it is rather short on specifics. During the life of Jesus, the veil is pulled back a bit, and we see more of Satan's activities. He tempts Jesus, possesses people, and enters Judas to lead the temple guards to the Garden of Gethsemane. In their letters, the apostles tell us that he is the "ruler of the kingdom of the air,"[98] the corrupter of the systems of the world, the one who will deceive and lead many in the last days. We read that he is a liar and the father of lies,[99] prowling around "like a roaring lion looking for someone to devour."[100] He is able to deceive people, appearing as an angel of light. They also tell us that, at some point, God will say, "Enough." At the right time in the Story, Jesus will return as a rider, fearless and true, and toss Satan and his followers into a lake of fire.

That is about all that we really know about the devil. What does it mean? Is Satan our principal antagonist? Is he the conflict that we must overcome? Is he the problem that Christ came to solve?

Perhaps Satan is merely an antagonistic character, not

the antagonist of our Story. He is a villain, for sure. He appears throughout the Story, from the time that he appears as the serpent in Eden. From time to time he comes to the forefront of the narrative, but he is always in the background, tempting, masquerading as foreign gods, afflicting people as an evil spirit, and so forth. But is he really the primary villain of the story that begins in the first two chapters of Genesis and ends in the last two chapters of Revelation? If Lucifer is not the antagonist, then who is?

A great story needs great conflict and an equally great antagonist. Does a great story really require the antagonist to be an individual, a personal villain? Let us consider two classic novels, Stephen Crane's *The Red Badge of Courage*[101] and Ernest Hemingway's *The Old Man the Sea*.[102] Those great stories "work" as well as any stories ever written. The nature of the conflict and the identity of the antagonist in them might give us clues to our own tale.

The Red Badge of Courage tells of a young soldier's first experience of battle in the American Civil War. The boy is bored working on his mother's farm, restless as he watches other local youths enlist and form a regiment. Like so many young men over the centuries, the uniforms, martial music, sense of adventure, and dreams of glory inspire him. Like so many other new soldiers throughout history he learns that war is more work than battle, that armies spend most of their time moving around, sitting around, building things, and living in camp. There is more that is dreary and ordinary about war than thrilling: long weeks of tedium punctuated by brief moments of sheer terror. As his unit finally maneuvers into position for its first experience of combat,[103] the young man's imagination begins to plague him. He wonders if he will be brave. He wonders if he will have the courage to hold the line in the face of the enemy volleys. He wonders what will happen to his body if it is pierced and shattered by an enemy mini-ball.

During the first day of the engagement, his company is overrun by an enemy charge and the young man breaks. He turns, drops his rifle, and runs far to the rear, into the forest. For a full day he wanders around. He gazes upon the Union dead and wounded. He walks among disorganized units and fresh reinforcements repositioning themselves according to the orders of the godlike generals who are able to see the bigger picture that lies beyond the view of the troops. To hide his embarrassment, he lies to his comrades about what happened to him. He is forced to confront his true self and to ask and answer questions about war, duty, loyalty, friendship, and belonging.

The second day of the battle is fiercer than the first. The youth finds something new in himself. He fights bravely, even heroically. He has changed, not because he defeats the Confederate soldiers, but because he defeats the weakness of his own character.

Who is the antagonist in this story? The Confederates? They are faceless shapes amidst smoke, noise, and the smell of cordite. Near the end of the story, after capturing an enemy position, the youth meets them for the first time. He finds them to be ordinary men, very much like himself. Is the antagonist the war itself, the generals, the violence?

No. The antagonist in *The Red Badge of Courage* is the

weak side of the youth's own nature. Folk religion likes to imagine that we each have a devil sitting on one shoulder and an angel on the other, debating what we ought to do. It is more accurate to say that we have two natures within us that struggle against each other. The apostle Paul described this conflict in his own life:

> I do not understand what I do. For what I want to do I do not do, but what I hate I do...I know that good itself does not dwell in me, that is, in my sinful nature. For I have the desire to do what is good, but I cannot carry it out. For I do not do the good I want to do, but the evil I do not want to do—this I keep on doing. Now if I do what I do not want to do, it is no longer I who do it, but it is sin living in me that does it...Although I want to do good, evil is right there with me. For in my inner being I delight in God's law; but I see another law at work in me, waging war against the law of my mind and making me a prisoner of the law of sin at work within me. What a wretched man I am![104]

The antagonist in *The Red Badge of Courage,* in Paul's story, in your and my stories, and in our shared Big Story, is our own fallen nature. Without a doubt, Satan takes advantage of our weakness: he tempts, harasses, oppresses, and—in some rare cases—even possesses us. He is an enemy, but our real enemy, the real source of conflict in our stories, is sin. This enemy takes two forms in our tale. Personal sin (our own rejection of God's goodness) is one face of our antagonist. Hemingway's story illustrates the other.

The Old Man and the Sea tells the story of Santiago, an elderly fisherman in pre-Revolutionary Cuba. When the story opens, Santiago has not caught a fish in eighty-four days. His neighbors consider Santiago unlucky, so much so that the parents of his young apprentice forbid him to fish with the old man any longer. Santiago tells the young man that tomorrow he intends to go deep into the Gulf to find a great catch to reverse his fortunes.

The next morning Santiago takes his small boat far from land. He sets his lines and after a few hours hooks a huge marlin. The fish is so large and powerful that Santiago cannot pull it in. Instead, it pulls the boat for two days and two nights across the ocean. For forty-eight hours Santiago bears the strain of the line with his body, afraid to let go. He is wounded, in great pain, and suffering from the effects of exposure to the elements.

Santiago respects his adversary, even feels compassion for the fish. He knows that this is a combat to the death. He is sad that one of them must not go home, and calls the fish his brother. On the third day of their struggle, the fish doubles back toward the boat and Santiago manages to kill it with a harpoon. The old man is depleted and delirious. He ties the marlin to the side of the boat and heads for shore. Santiago thinks about how much money he will earn in the market and how many people the great fish will feed.

By this point the bleeding carcass is attracting sharks. Santiago kills one with his harpoon, but loses the harpoon in the process. He improvises a spear from his knife and an oar, and he fights off more of the swarming fins. Through the night the sharks attack, far beyond his ability to defend. They gnaw at the marlin's body, and by the time he reaches shore the next morning there is nothing left of the great fish but a skeleton dragging behind the boat. He collapses into his bed, exhausted. While he sleeps, the local fisher-men measure the bones—all Santiago has to show for his four-day journey—and are amazed at the size of the marlin.

Who is the antagonist in *The Old Man and the Sea?* The marlin? The sharks? The sea? Santiago's age and pov-erty, which drive him so far into the open ocean?

In the third chapter of Genesis God sentenced Santiago, and us, to a life of hard labor:

> To Adam he said, "Because you listened to your wife and
> ate fruit from the tree about which I commanded you, 'You
> must not eat from it,'
> "Cursed is the ground because of you;
> through painful toil you will eat food from it
> all the days of your life.
> It will produce thorns and thistles for you,
> and you will eat the plants of the field.
> By the sweat of your brow
> you will eat your food
> until you return to the ground,
> since from it you were taken;
> for dust you are
> and to dust you will return."[105]

Because Adam and Eve rejected God's protection and blessing, Santiago and we face the endless human struggle to earn a living in a world that gives us nothing for free. The curse of Adam has made working our way through this world hard. Whether you fish or farm, build or bake, write sales orders or books, this world constantly grinds you down. We are filled with anxiety about our food, shelter, and clothing.[106] While this anxiety and effort could and should drive us toward God, far too often it drives us deeper into sin. We do not trust God, and so we lie, cheat, steal, hoard, envy, fight, manipulate, abuse, abandon, despair, control, and kill. The road through the valley of the shadow of death [107] is bumpy and dangerous, but it always leads downhill to the grave. [108]

Satan is our enemy. Make no mistake of that. We are God's creation, bearing his image, and Satan tries to vandalize us. We are God's children, and Satan tries to molest and corrupt us. We are God's agents, stewards, and instruments, and Satan tries to render us impotent and unfruitful. We must always be on guard against his depredations. The apostle Peter warned:

> Be alert and of sober mind. Your enemy the devil prowls around like a roaring lion looking for someone to devour. Resist him, standing firm in the faith, because you know that the family of believers throughout the world is undergoing the same kind of sufferings. [109]

Let us give this enemy just the right amount of credit: not too little, but certainly not too much. He understands the Big Story and our struggle better than we do. He knows how this game works, he knows our vulnerabilities, and you had better believe that he is keeping score. In fact, the very word "Satan" means "the Accuser" in Hebrew. He is the one who stands before God, accusing us of our sin. [110] This is the point: it is our sin that separates us from God, which drags us ever downward into the pit, and against which we struggle. It is our ultimate adversary.

Which leads us to an obvious next question: who is the protagonist in our Story?

- chapter 16 -

The Protagonist

In 47 BC, Julius Caesar and his legions had just put down an uprising in Egypt when they landed on the southern coast of modern-day Turkey. They were on their way back to Rome, where Caesar had a restless Senate to contend with. Upon landing, the general got word that Pharnaces, the king of Pontus, had rebelled against Roman authority near the Black Sea and had taken control of a large swath of Armenia. Caesar split off a relatively small portion of his forces and quickly marched north to a place called Zile, where he found Pharnaces' army. The experienced legionnaires won victory on the field in just five hours, pacifying the Black Sea region under Roman control. Caesar then pivoted westward, back toward Rome, and sent a dispatch ahead to the Senate. It was only one sentence, of three words: "*Veni, Vidi, Vici.*" In English, it reads, "I came, I saw, I conquered."

I know a better story. Its opening sentence makes a small change in grammar that makes a huge difference for all of us: *venit, vidit, vicit.*

Buddhism is one of the world's great religions. It is always perilous to summarize a worldview into a few words, especially one that has multiple branches, with diverse traditions and teachings. If we were to try, we might say that Buddhism rests on three premises:

- Life is full of pain, suffering, and error.
- There is nothing that you or I can do to change this.
- Enlightenment, therefore, comes from accepting and rising above the pain and suffering of this life. In a sense, we must get used to it.

Christianity agrees with the first two of Buddhism's premises. Undeniably, life is full of pain, suffering, and error. There is nothing that you or I can do to change the nature of the world. Where Christianity and Buddhism part ways is the third premise: Christianity teaches that we do not have to get used to it. We should never accept the brokenness of the cosmos, because we know someone who can—and has, and will—change everything.

Venit. He came.

The Christian New Testament was written in Greek. In it, the word *parousia* is used a couple dozen times, in the sense of someone coming to or arriving at a place. In quite a few places it is used in sentences discussing Jesus' eventual return to earth. Some Christians refer to this future second coming of Jesus as "the Parousia."

The medieval Church in Western Europe spoke Latin. The Latin word for "coming" or "arrival" is *adventus,* and thus the Church began to celebrate the four weeks before

Christmas as "Advent," the season that celebrates Jesus' first coming.

The first-coming Advent and the second-coming Parousia are part of the baffling and wonderful arc of the Big Story. Depending on where we are in the pages, those events might be in the past, present, or future. When the Story is over, this will be the bottom line: he came, he is here, and he has always been here.

One day, Jesus and his disciples were crossing the Sea of Galilee in a fishing boat. Jesus was tired, and fell asleep in the bottom of the boat. A terrible storm arose and the wind tossed the waves so high that the boat was in danger of being capsized. Seemingly oblivious, Jesus kept napping. The terrified disciples shook him awake, asking if he even cared that they were about to drown. Jesus was irritated. He stood and shouted at the wind and waves, telling them to shut up and let him rest. Instantly, the storm abated and the sea was calm. The disciples were amazed and asked, "What kind of man is this? Even the winds and the waves obey him!"[111]

Indeed. Just who was the guy in the boat?

John tells us[112] that in the beginning was the Word (logos), that the Word was with God, and that the Word was God. He goes on to say that through the Word, all things (the cosmos) were made, and nothing has been made that was not made through him. In his letter to the Colossians, Paul tells us that through Christ all things (the cosmos) were created by him and for him, and that in him all things hold together.[113]

He has always been a part of this Story. From the beginning, his character was infused into the fabric of the world. He moved upon the waters, dividing them from the dry land. He scooped up the star stuff, the raw material of our planet, and blew into it the breath of life.

He has moved freely throughout the Story, a constant presence, an occasional character, and a perpetual mystery. He walked as a flame between Abraham's sacrificed animals, binding himself in a covenant with his people.[114] Later, Abraham cooked him lunch by the oaks of Mamre, and tried to persuade him to spare the cities of Sodom and Gomorrah.[115] Elijah heard his still, small voice when the prophet hid in a cave in the wilderness with a price on his head.[116] He stood in the fiery furnace, chatting with Shadrach, Meshach, and Abednego.[117] The guy in the boat has always been a part of our story.

When the Old Testament prophets looked forward, they did not distinguish between *adventus* and *parousia*, between first and second coming. They simply foresaw a time when he would arrive, and everything would change.

He came. He has never really left, but he will step onto the stage again at the end of the Story. During his *adventus*, his first big scene as a flesh and blood character on the pages of our Story, he changed everything. It is the nexus, the crux, and the turning point of the entire Story. He came.

Vedit. He saw.

As a character, written onto and living beside us on the pages of our Story, he saw life as we see it. Much has been said about the humble beginnings and life of Jesus as a carpenter's son in a small village. One thing I have wondered about, though: did he have a foreign accent? He spent some part of his childhood living in Egypt, hiding from King Herod. When he returned to Nazareth, did the other children in the village see him as an outsider? Did anyone question or subtly sneer about his mother being pregnant before the wedding? The strange rumors surrounding his birth? His years abroad? Did the other kids notice an Egyptian accent? Did he know the pain of the playground, the criticism of his peers? It would have been a foreshadowing of what was to come in his story. Isaiah had foretold that he would be "despised and rejected by mankind, a man of suffering, and familiar with pain. Like one from whom people hide their faces...and [held] in low esteem."[118]

He had younger siblings, so he probably helped care for them. Most likely, he changed a diaper or two, helped fix meals. He appears to have lost his father by the time he was grown, and so he had to become the man of the house. He almost certainly knew financial pressure and the stress of feeding a family (there is no reason to think he just miraculously put dinner on the table every night). He knew about taxes (one of his disciples was the town tax collector), and awkward social moments (his relatives ran out of wine at a wedding). His cousin John was arrested and beheaded, and his friend Lazarus died. Jesus wept.

He came, but he did not hover over our heads like some otherworldly guru, or glide through our world like a ghost, or retreat from ordinary life like an enlightened Buddha. He saw our life from our vantage point, lost in the pages.

He saw.

Vicit. He Conquered.

The Author wrote himself into his own Story. It is the pivot upon which the entire plot turns.

The first Adam broke the world. To restore it, Adam's failure had to be reversed. For reasons that are still not clear, the Author tied the condition of the cosmos to the condition of humanity. As long as humans bore a genetic defect, with decay and death coded into our DNA, the universe would be held in bondage. Our disease was a cancer spreading through the universe, corroding it from the inside out. Tossing us a lifeline, putting salve on our wounds, or even allowing us an escape to heaven would not be enough. The root of the problem had to be dealt with. The world had to be fixed, once and for all.

So the second person of the Trinity, the one who had always been here, came onstage as a character. *Adventus.* He became a second Adam. Like a traveler lost among endless side roads, he would go back to the point where we made the wrong turn off the highway. He would take Adam and Eve's test again, and not fail it this time.

He obeyed. He was tempted in every way that we are, yet he did not sin. Decay and death got no foothold in his life. Therefore, just as death came to all men through Adam,[119] so life can come through Jesus. The last enemy to be put down is death, and he has begun that process.[120] Death has lost its sting. It is being unraveled. He has not left the Story, but when he comes back on stage for his final scene, death and decay will lay down their arms and surrender.

Like Caesar at Zile, he put down humanity's rebellion quickly. He conquered. We are living through the mop-up, as the last insurgents are being rooted out.

A Roman triumph was an honor bestowed by the Senate on victorious generals. It consisted of a parade through the streets of Rome, with the glorious commander basking in the adulation of the crowd, while behind him trailed captives, prisoners of war who had become slaves, the spoils of war. When Caesar returned to Rome after defeating Pharnaces at Zile, he received a triumph. His one-sentence report from the front was considered so clever and dashing, even by his contemporaries, that the banners carried before Caesar had *Vini, Vidi, Vici* written on them.

Christ received a triumph as well. He "ascended on high, leading captives in his train."[121] Only these were not unfortunate prisoners of war from the other side, they were those of us who had been captive to decay and death, whom he set free. We follow in his triumph, not sullen and intimidated by having been captured, but smiling in bewilderment and blinking as our prison eyes adjust to the light of a renewed cosmos.

There is a curious scene in the fifth chapter of Revelation. It illustrates, through symbol and metaphor, the role of Christ as the central protagonist of the Big Story and the pivotal figure in the turning of its plot.

The apostle John was given a vision of the throne room of God the Father, the Author of the Big Story. The one seated on the throne held a scroll in his right hand, with writing on both sides and sealed with seven wax seals.

What is this scroll? Some Christians have suggested that it is the text of the Bible, or a sentence of judgment against God's enemies, or even the deed to planet Earth, among other things. Most think that it is God's will, his plan, for the universe. I believe that it is the Big Story, his will expressed as the great narrative of the cosmos. It records what has been, what is, and what shall be. The scroll has writing on both sides because the Story is so dense, so rich, and so expansive. It is sealed with seven different seals, which is the number of God, indicating that only the Author can open and unleash this tale. Only he can bring it to life.

An angel, a member of the divine court, asked in a loud voice if anyone was worthy to break the seals and open the scroll. But there was no one on earth or under the earth (living or dead) that could open the scroll or even look inside of it. No creature—no character in the Story—is able to unlock or unleash the Story, to move it forward to completion. John says that he wept because there was no one that could bring this tale to life. We are merely words on a scroll, unless someone can animate us and make the words come true. John breaks down: he says that he wept and wept, his tears falling and his heart rending to realize that there is no character good enough and strong enough to make us real. Search history, scour all the little stories, rifle through all the aspirations of humanity and all the pretension of empires, and there is still no one and no thing that can bring us to life. John cried, his heart broken, and so should we.

Then another member of the divine court, a deceased

saint, consoled John. "Do not weep! See, the Lion of the tribe of Judah, the Root of David, has triumphed. He is able to open the scroll and its seven seals." Then John looked, and saw a lamb that looked as if it had been slain. This was Jesus, who was foreshadowed in the story of Israel by the annual Passover lamb. After his resurrection he still bore the scars of his crucifixion. All the story lines converge in him. He approached the throne and took the scroll from the right hand of the Author.

Then the throne room was filled with a cacophony of praise. Characters of all sorts—human, angelic, and other-worldly—cried out that he, the lamb of God, the lion of Judah, the first century Roman provincial Jew, Jesus bar-Joseph, was worthy to take the scroll and to open its seals, because he was slain! He alone is able to roll out God's Story for the cosmos. Because he became a character himself, he is able to bring the rest of us to life. He is able to make us, and our little stories, real. He conquered.

He came, he saw, and he conquered. Enlightenment is not accepting and rising above the pain, suffering, and error of this world. It is to be given life, by the only one who can make the Story, written by the Ancient of Days, come true.

chapter 17

The Thorn and The Rose

Der Ring des Nibelungen ("The Ring of the Nibelung") is a series of four epic operas by the German composer Richard Wagner (1813-1883). They are loosely based on characters from Norse mythology, and are often referred to as "The Ring Cycle," "Wagner's Ring," or simply "The Ring."

It is art on an huge scale. As written, it is fifteen hours long (Wagner intended it to be performed over four nights). The story is epic: three generations of gods, heroes, and mythical creatures struggle to control a magic ring that grants domination over the entire world.[122] The climactic performance, *Götterdämmerung* ("The Twilight of the Gods"), illustrates the end of the world, as told in Norse mythology.

Wagner realized that a fifteen-hour opera would test the audience's attention span and that all the characters and subplots might be confusing. His solution was to write certain melodies or harmonic progressions that would be linked to particular characters or elements and would play whenever the appropriate person or thing appeared on-stage. They serve as cues: when we hear one of these melodies we know what is happening and how we should respond (cheer for the good guy or fear the bad guy).

Wagner called these musical themes *leitmotifs*. It was not a new technique; other composers had done similar things. Writers of literature have long used certain words, phrases, or iconic elements as clues and cues for the reader. But Wagner took the use of leitmotifs to a new level in Western music.

All this raises an interesting question: does our Big Story use leitmotifs to make us aware of what is going on in the narrative and how we should respond? Should we be looking for recurring patterns in life and nature that hint at bigger themes? If so, what are they? Are there any master motifs that stand out? I believe there are. In our Story, two of those iconic elements are a thorn and a rose.

In his second letter to the church at Corinth, Paul mentions his thorn. He does not tell us what it is; only that it is. The ambiguity only makes it more iconic, more of a representative element for the rest of us:

> To keep me from becoming conceited because of these surpassingly great revelations, there was given me a thorn in my flesh, a messenger of Satan, to torment me. Three times I pleaded with the Lord to take it away from me. But he said to me, "My grace is sufficient for you, for my power is made perfect in weakness." Therefore I will boast all the more gladly about my weaknesses, so that Christ's power may rest on me. That is why, for Christ's sake, I delight in weaknesses, in insults, in hardships, in persecutions, in difficulties. For when I am weak, then I am strong.[123]

What is your thorn? What does God plague you with? A

weakness in your body? In your character? A persistent temptation or addiction? Why? What purpose does it serve in your life, other than to break your heart and frustrate your existence?[124] Paul recognized that the Author had written the thorn into his life as a subplot; it punctured his smugness and overconfidence. What does your thorn puncture in you?

Running in and out of our big and little stories, the thorn is a leitmotif that reminds us not to be satisfied with the way things are. The word "sin" has several meanings. The first meaning that comes to our mind is personal, moral sin: bad things that we do. Sin is more than that. Cultures, systems, and civilizations can also be sinful. It is not just that they do bad things, but that they are fundamentally flawed. Even the physical universe suffers the effects of sin.[125]

The doctrine of *total depravity* is misunderstood. It does not mean that everyone, or everything, is as bad as they possibly could be. That is obviously not true, for there is love and beauty in the world. Instead, total depravity means that nothing is untouched by sin. It is a genetic defect we are all born with, affecting our DNA and our universe at the molecular level. Everything we build is subject to rust and crumble. Every group or system—families, nations, churches—are subject to perversion and corruption. The original sin in the Garden of Eden stained everything.[126]

In this Story, our thorns are personal reminders that no matter our intentions or ambitions, sin lurks close at hand. The apostle Paul was as devoted to Christ as anyone. He was used by the Spirit to take the Gospel to the Gentiles and to write much of the New Testament, and was given "surpassingly great revelations."[127] With all of that, he could easily have lost the plot, become conceited, and forgotten what the Story was all about. Like one of the leitmotifs in Wagner's Ring, Paul's thorn trots out onstage and sings an ominous melody. Sin cannot be ignored.

God speaks to us in the Bible through many different genres: narrative, poetry, proverbs, epistles, and more. One of the most unique and unexpected is semi-erotic love poetry.

The Old Testament book Song of Songs, also called the Song of Solomon, is an extended, poetic dialogue between a king and his new bride. They talk about their love for each other, including their physical love. In the second chapter, the woman says to the king, "I am a rose of Sharon, a lily of the valleys."[128]

That is a beautiful thing to say, but what is it doing in the Bible? Most of us have pet names for our loved ones. What is the point of including pillow talk in the Holy Scriptures?

Love is the dominant strain, the underlying melody, and the foundational plot line of our Story. It is often buried below subplots, hidden beneath layers of discordant sound. It is always there. Every now and then it breaks through, rises over the surface of the troubled waters, and reminds us what this Story is all about.

It is important to understand the subject, verb, and object of our love. No one could look at our little stories, or the bigger story of our world, and conclude that our love for each other was the theme of this world. Our capacity and propensity for love is occasional, capricious and tepid—at best. We do not give it or receive it consistently. When we do love, it is too often tainted with self-interest. No, the dominant theme of the Big Story is that we *are* loved, in spite of our being only marginally loving and lovable. Love is the verb, but in this Story we are its object, not its subject. Our rose is the constant reminder that God loves us.

At one level, the Song of Songs is a model for marriage. It is a template for how we should treasure the mate that God has given us. At a deeper level, it is an illustration of the relationship between Christ and his people. Deeper yet, it may teach us something about how the Creator feels about his creation. We are the beloved. We are the rose. The rose does not inspire us; it should humble us before his unconditional and self-sacrificial devotion to those unwilling and unable to return it.

We do not understand love very well. We have one English word "love" that has too many duties in our daily conversation. We use it to describe all sorts of feelings, actions, and relationships. We love doughnuts. We get that loving feeling, and we make love. We love NY, we love LA, we love the USA. Paris is a city of love. We fall in love and fall out of love. We know Jesus loves us, and sometimes we even love him back. We are surrounded by love. Love is in the air (especially on Valentine's and Mother's Days).

So, why are we not happier? Knee-deep in all this love, why are our families so fragile? Why is there so little peace in our churches, much less our world?

Most of what we call love is really attraction, attachment, fondness, or desire. All of these are important parts of what it means to be human. God help us if we have to do without them. But they are not the rose in our Story. At best they are rosebuds: hints and foreshadowing of a rich, full bloom to come.

The rose is stronger stuff. It is also more distant. It is like the horns of Elfland: we think that we hear them in the woods at night, accompanied by flickering lights that might be a hunt for a white stag. We think that we hear them on a breeze, carried over a not-too-distant hill on a summer afternoon, and our heart breaks to think that if we could only run over the next crest fast enough we might find our way into a better world, with better things that have always just eluded us.

The rose in our Story is like that. We catch glimpses of it, we get an occasional taste, and we hear a few bars of its melody break through before it is drowned out by all the noise of ordinary life. The rose in our Story is the love that we long for, which pierces our heart, that gives us hope (and that we sometimes oddly despise), but is far too rare. It is an otherworldly love, an alien thing, but it is the only shape that fills the deepest hole in us; we want to hear our Creator say, "I love you."

We can hear that. We have to learn to listen, but if we do we will hear it in his still, small voice. We will hear it in the great movements of nature, in the kindness of strangers, in the blessings of hearth and home. Over and over and over—if we pay attention—we will hear him say, "Yes, you are my rose of Sharon, my lily of the valleys. Like a lily among the thorns."

In our Story, the thorn and the rose are inseparable. We are drawn to the rose, but to enjoy it deeply and often, our conceit and complacency must be regularly punctured. Our fallen flesh carries many forms of the disease: pride, lust, envy, conceit, gluttony, and far too many more. The thorn in our lives is there to keep the sickness at bay, and ultimately to lance the boil, excise the tumor, remove the stench of sin from our nostrils. Only then can we deeply inhale the rose.

Part IV

And They All Lived...

- chapter 18 -

Joy

I suppose that I am a bad parent, because sometimes I let my kids have ice cream for dinner. It is a tradition in our family. Not far from our house is a walk-up ice cream shack, with wooden tables and benches under huge oaks. The place is a local landmark, and on summer evenings folks are lined up ten deep for the signature sundaes. About once a week during the warm months, my wife and I look at each other and ask, "Ice cream for dinner tonight?" We take the kids, or the kids and their friends, and cover all the essential food groups: salt and protein (in the pecans), dairy, sugar, fat, and fruit (the cherry on top of the mountain of whipped cream). And chocolate, of course, which is a necessary brick in any sane food pyramid.

I am ashamed to admit that I never keep my end of the bargain, though. We get home from the sundae place at seven thirty on those summer evenings, and by ten o'clock I'm rummaging through the refrigerator, looking for real food. To be honest, I did not have ice cream for dinner, I just had dessert first. Ice cream makes me happy, but it does not leave me satisfied, so I am left wanting more—something substantial, something with weight, something that sustains.

That is how I feel about happy endings to stories. I am glad to hear that the characters lived happily ever after, but I want more, and I suspect that the characters do, as well. Happy stories are great, but they feel like ice cream for dinner.

I have a friend who is a screenwriter, and sometimes he speaks to groups about Christian movies.[129] He does a little test: he asks people if they were given free tickets to a premiere of a new "Christian" movie, how many of those present would bother to go. Surprisingly, even in churches, not many hands go up. They give plenty of reasons for why they would pass on the opportunity, but one theme that emerges is that people expect "Christian" movies to be happy movies, with happy endings. Quite a few people are bored by the very idea. It's ice cream for dinner.

I feel the same way about many Christian books. They seem too focused on happiness. Of course they contain conflict (whether novels or nonfiction), but the conflict is usually a challenge to the characters' happiness. The worldview of these stories seems to assume that Christians ought to be happy, but that various sins and a corrupt world disrupt their bliss in Christ. If they would only surrender to Jesus, get properly involved in a local church, and surround themselves with other followers of Christ, then the waters would calm and they could live happily ever after. It makes me happy as a reader to know that the characters are happy, but these books leave me unsatisfied, wanting more. They feel like ice cream for dinner.

The stories in the Bible are not like that. They rarely, if ever, are concerned with happiness. The biblical stories play for higher stakes. They are about joy.

God promised Abram that he would be the father of many, and that a great nation would come from his body.[130] He went where he was told, believed God, and it was credited to him as righteousness. He got benefits, too: he was rich and powerful, with thousands of cattle and hundreds of servants. But he had no children. The decades went by and the pain became more acute. His wife Sarah felt worthless. She assumed that it was her fault that she could not conceive and provide Abram the heir he deserved.

In a fit of desperation, she offered her servant Hagar to her husband, telling him to sleep with her as a surrogate wife to produce a child that Sarah could raise. It was a bad idea for all sorts of reasons, but they were old, getting older, and desperate for a solution. Hagar got pregnant and gave birth to a child they named Ishmael. Meanwhile, the angel of the Lord had visited Abram and Sarah and repeated his promise to provide a child through them. The angel said that she would bear a child within the following year. At this point Sarah was old, well past the point where this was humanly possible. She laughed bitterly at the angel. A year later, she held a new baby, whom God told them to name Isaac, meaning "laughter." The boy's name was a living rebuttal to her disbelief and scorn of God's promise. Of course, there was now a rather awkward family dynamic: Ishmael was the first, but he was the unwanted half-child of Sarah's servant. Sarah wanted Hagar and Ishmael, a rival for her boy's place and inheritance, gone. So she had them driven into the wilderness. They were forever separated from the blessings promised to the family. Isaac was an only child, and eventually he had children of his own, but Sarah and Abram never lived to see their grandchildren. They did not all live happily ever after, but God did bring them joy. It's weighty stuff, not ice cream for dinner.

Their great-grandchildren could not get along.[131] The youngest, Joseph, was a gifted child, his dad's favorite, and kind of a show-off. His brothers found him irritating, and one day they faked his death and sold him into slavery. Their father Jacob mourned over the clothing that they had stained with sheep's blood, thinking it was proof of his beloved son's demise. Many years went by. Everyone got older, and they lived through hard times. What they did not know was that Joseph had, with God's help, risen from the dungeons of Egypt to become the prime minister, second-in-command to Pharaoh himself. Joseph managed the affairs of state so competently that Egypt had agricultural reserves when a famine struck the eastern Mediterranean region.

Meanwhile, back in Israel, Joseph's father was desperate, and he sent a couple of his remaining sons to Egypt to buy some grain. Joseph recognized his brothers, although they did not recognize him. He demanded that they bring their father (and his, although they did not realize it) and the rest of the brothers back to him before he would make the sale. In the end, he wept to see his aged father, and he revealed himself. There was restoration and forgiveness in the family, but there had been so much pain and so many wasted years that it was bittersweet. They did not all live happily ever after, but God did bring them joy. The story is weighty stuff, not ice cream for dinner.

Many centuries later, a woman named Hannah was childless.[132] Her life felt as barren as her womb. She went to the tabernacle of the Lord, pouring out her grief and begging God for a child. The priest, Eli, saw her mumbling and scolded her for coming to the sanctuary intoxicated. But she was not murmuring drunken rubbish, she was doing what so many of us do in our pain and longing: bargaining with God. If the Lord would only validate her life by giving her a child, she promised to give the child up to be raised as a priest in God's tabernacle. She would have the blessing of bearing and suckling a child, even if he was taken from her in boyhood to live among the Levites. At least she would be able to say with pride that her son had an important job. God granted her request, and the boy Samuel grew up away from his mother, living among the priests. He became a great man, and no doubt Hannah died satisfied. They did not all live happily ever after, but God did bring them joy. The story is weighty stuff, not ice cream for dinner.

Many centuries later, a man who had been crippled from birth was healed by the name of Jesus. No one gave him a pension or reimbursed him for the years that he had lain in the dirt, begging from those on their way into the temple.[133] A woman was caught in the act of adultery and dragged, perhaps half-naked, into the street by a mob with stones in their hands. A traveling rabbi defused the situation and the stones were dropped. She was told to go and sin no more.[134] Another woman, whose sins were many, barged into a posh dinner party and wept on the same rabbi's feet, washing them with her hair. To the offense of everyone there, he raised her chin and told her gently that she was forgiven. She slipped away, into the night.[135] John, the "disciple that Jesus loved,"[136] outlived his colleagues, but spent his last years as an exile on a rocky Greek island. He was a very, very old man when the last things were revealed to him in a vision. None of these people lived happily ever after, but God did bring them joy. Their stories are weighty stuff, not ice cream for dinner.

Happiness and joy are not synonyms. Happiness is dessert first, but joy is a wedding banquet. It is about what is lost as well as what is gained. A wedding banquet celebrates love and possibility and finding the heart's desires, but it also requires moving from childhood and the protection of parents to new homes and new responsibilities. People cry at weddings. They are tears of joy, but they are not all tears of happiness. Joy is a meal that sustains, that satisfies our deepest longings. Joy is tinged with loss and sadness. Joy is happiness that has been bought with a price, sometimes at a terrible cost. Joy is happiness with worth. Happiness is nice, but joy is precious.

If stories with happy endings are ice cream for dinner, then the Lord's Supper is a joyful meal. Paid for with the body and blood of *Immanuel* ("God with Us" in Hebrew), it is the most expensive meal you will ever eat. But you don't pick up the tab. It has been completely paid for by the man at the head of the table. As you take the elements, you taste joy in material form. No one lives happily ever after when they are united with the body and blood of Jesus, for we are marked with his sufferings and live in this world, which he has overcome but not subdued. Holy Communion is a joyful union with Christ, but it is not ice cream for dinner. No one is left hungry. Sometimes, when I am serving communion in a gathering of God's people, I see those who hang back and chose not to take it. There are many reasons why they might do that, and before breaking the bread I advise everyone to abstain under certain conditions. Still, I wonder where they are in their stories. Are they refusing joy because they are holding out for happiness?

I confess a natural inclination to sad stories. I like bittersweet tales and bittersweet music. I get goose bumps when I sense genuine joy in a story, but I savor the melancholy of the pains the characters endure to find it. I can listen to Celtic ballads about life on hard but beautiful landscapes all day long. I cry like a baby when Aslan tells the characters at the end of *The Chronicles of Narnia* that they have died in a train crash, or when Frodo reaches the Gray Havens at the end of *The Lord of the Rings*. These are not happy endings, but they are joyful endings.

It seems to me that the Author of our stories, of our Story, is more concerned with joy than happiness. That is how he ends his tales. Thomas touches the risen Jesus' scars. They are proof that the joy of Easter was costly. Peter leaps from the boat and swims to the beach to be reunited with the master that he denied three times. After breakfast, Peter is grieved when Jesus questions the depth of his love and tells him that he will someday be led to his own execution. According to church tradition, Peter was crucified in the imperial gardens of Rome by Emperor Nero. We are told that he asked to be crucified upside down, because he was not worthy to die in the same manner as his Lord.

I cried when I wrote that last sentence. That is a joyful ending, not a happy one.

So will our own ending be. Revelation 22—nearly the last words in the Bible—assures us that in the city where God dwells with his people in the restored cosmos, the main street is lined with the Trees of Life. The Lord put an angel with a flaming sword to keep us out of Eden after the Fall, lest we eat from that very tree and live forever alienated from him. In the end, we are told, it will bear enough fruit to heal the nations.[137]

We are not guaranteed a happy ending. God does not serve ice cream for dinner. We are promised something far better: joy.

chapter 19

Tell Your Story

The protagonist of Charles Frazier's 1997 novel *Cold Mountain* is a wounded soldier named Inman who deserts from the Confederate army. At the height of the Civil War, he walks home through hundreds of miles of the war-torn South. He comes across plenty of people that are suffering the costs of war, but none struck me as much as one young widow that Inman meets in a remote cabin, high in the mountains. She is an eighteen-year-old girl with a two-year-old baby. Her husband was killed in the war "up in Virginia." She and the child are starving, unable to maintain the meager farm. Hidden in a little valley, her hunger is made worse by loneliness. Inman slaughters a hog for her, and she prepares him a meal. She gives him some of her husband's clothes to replace his rags. He lies down to sleep in the corncrib, but during the night she comes out and invites him into the cabin. Inman is unsure of her intentions, but she asks him if he would be able to lie beside her without making any sexual advances. She just wants to feel another body next to her. He agrees, and lies in her bed fully clothed. By the light of fire, she whispers her memories. Frazier writes, "She required of Inman only that he bear witness to her tale. Every time he went to speak she said, 'Hush.' There was nothing remarkable about her story other than that it was her life."[138]

That last sentence moves me. Does it not ring true? Do we not need someone to bear witness to our tale? For most of us, there nothing remarkable about our story other than that it is ours. It is the only story we will ever have.

In my work, I hear lots of people's stories. Most of them are not newsworthy. They will never be published, and no studio will buy the movie rights. But all of them matter.

Many of us believe that our story does not matter unless it is a grand drama, an engaging comedy, a fascinating documentary, or an epic tragedy. We consider our lives unworthy of note unless we are heroes or the long-suffering victims of great injustice. Some folks exaggerate or invent better stories about themselves. Others keep their mouths shut, sure that their tale is too dull to tell. Many of us leave out inconvenient details that would undermine the narrative we are trying to sell.

We have it all wrong: our stories matter because of what they reveal about the Big Story. There are patterns, connections, hints, and clues, underground rivers and veins and currents of meaning that run through our lives. Modern psychology has it backwards; our stories are not portals down into the caverns of our minds, full of swirling chemicals and firing synapses. Instead, they are vantage points from which to watch the movement of the larger narrative and to hear what the Author is trying to tell us through it.

During the seventeenth century, a small community of European philosophers began arguing about whether any of them could prove that he existed. From the outside, it seems weird and pointless. It was the sort of conversation that only makes sense if you have been following closely and understand the context. René Descartes, a French mathematician and philosopher, offered the most famous suggestion for how to verify that one is actually real. He began by admitting that the world around him—the earth, other people, even his own body—could be an illusion, fed to him by a powerful demon. What could he be absolutely sure of? His bottom line was this: "I think, therefore I am."[139] In other words, his mind must exist, otherwise how could he wonder about his own existence?

Although Descartes and his colleagues would argue that it might be an illusion, the only thing that gives our existence meaning is our story. We were here. We saw, heard, and felt. We met people and visited places. We fought and loved, gave and stole. We are witnesses to this world. The philosophers have miscalculated: to be human is not to contemplate and reason; it is to have a story. "To be" is to be a character in the history of this world. I have story, therefore I am.

Your story is the only thing that is really yours. It is who you are. It defines you, gives you identity and place and purpose. Your story is the Author's gift to you. He gave you a role in the Big Story. If it does not feel like a pleasant or worthy role, it is still inescapably who you are. Your story has value because it gives us another perspective, another voice, another data point from which we can grasp the larger plot and hear the Author's voice. Your real story, the story you must learn well enough to tell, is not about you at all. It is your part in the Story. It happens in and through and around you, but you are not the point.

Telling your story is not the same as talking about yourself. More shameless narcissism is not the cure to what ails our world. Some of us do not need much of a nudge to start going on and on about what we find fascinating about ourselves, ignoring the body language of listeners looking for an exit. Most of us know someone who has told us the same boring stories about their life so many times that we could recite them ourselves. We do not need any more promotional hagiographies about politicians, rock stars, or athletes. We need to stop making it all about us, because it is not.

Telling our story—if we tell the truth—sheds the first and most insidious of the consequences of our Fall: the impulse to hide. Adam and Eve came into the world naked and unashamed. They had no secrets, for there was nothing to keep secret. Without pockets, robes, or veils they had nowhere to conceal anything even if they had wanted to. The very first thing they did after their eyes were opened[140] was cover up and then hide in the shrubbery. In their first conversation with God afterward, they began the obfuscation and evasion that plague our lives. What did they tell their children about why they left Eden? How honest was their story? Their first-born son seemed to learn how to hide the truth (and the body) pretty quickly.[141] When we tell our story truthfully we begin to unravel what Sir Walter Scott called, "The tangled web we weave when first we practice to deceive."[142]

Zerrubabel learned truth about his story from Zechariah.

Around 600 BC, the Babylonians sacked Jerusalem. They pillaged and burned, and they destroyed the temple of the Lord that Solomon had built. They carted off many of the best and brightest of the city's youth to captivity in the East. They left a city without a wall, ruined, and exposed. The Lord had told the Israelites that he would do this, and he was true to his word. After that, he sent the Persians to conquer the Babylonians. The Jewish exiles fell under the rule of Cyrus the Great.

Then the story took another twist: the Author had Cyrus agree to let some of the exiles return and rebuild. Nehemiah had become his cupbearer, and Cyrus not only gave him permission to raise the walls of Jerusalem but he funded the project as well. Zerrubabel was in that first wave of exiles to come home to the City of David. He was a Persian official of Jewish descent, and Cyrus the Great appointed him governor of Jerusalem. Once he got there, he conceived a plan to rebuild the destroyed temple. He and his colleagues began assembling the resources:

> Then they gave money to the masons and carpenters, and gave food and drink and olive oil to the people of Sidon and Tyre, so that they would bring cedar logs by sea from Lebanon to Joppa, as authorized by Cyrus king of Persia. In the second month of the second year after their arrival at the house of God in Jerusalem, Zerubbabel son of Shealtiel, Joshua son of Jozadak and the rest of the people

(the priests and the Levites and all who had returned from the captivity to Jerusalem) began the work.[143]

The work went well, and the rebuilt temple had a profound effect on the residents of Jerusalem. It was bittersweet, as joy often is, because it had come at such a cost. The people were elated that Zerrubabel was rebuilding the temple, but they could not help but to think of all that had been lost by the nation's turning away from the Lord: not just lives, but innocence and integrity. Everyone assembled to celebrate the laying of the new foundation, and at the climax of the ceremony

> all the people gave a great shout of praise to the LORD, because the foundation of the house of the LORD was laid. But many of the older priests and Levites and family heads, who had seen the former temple, wept aloud when they saw the foundation of this temple being laid, while many others shouted for joy. No one could distinguish the sound of the shouts of joy from the sound of weeping, because the people made so much noise. And the sound was heard far away.[144]

We do not know how Zerrubabel might have told his story if someone had asked him to on that day. For that matter, we do not know how the people celebrating the dedication of the foundation of the new temple might have told their stories. It is likely that they would have related all they had lived through: captivity, hardship, return, risk, and hard work. I say that because of the message that God sent, which seems like a cautionary reminder that what had happened was not all about them.

There was a prophet named Zechariah in Jerusalem at

the time. The Lord gave him a message to send to the governor, celebrating what they had accomplished. As Zechariah recorded it, "So he said to me, 'This is the word of the LORD to Zerubbabel: 'Not by might nor by power, but by my Spirit,' says the LORD Almighty.'" [145] Zerrubabel did not rebuild the temple because he was clever, or industrious, or bold, or a great administrator. Certainly, Zerrubabel was all of those things. That was his character's role, but his story was propelled by the Author's initiative. As another prophet, named Haggai, recorded it, "So the LORD stirred up the spirit of Zerubbabel son of Shealtiel, governor of Judah, and the spirit of Joshua son of Jozadak, the high priest, and the spirit of the whole remnant of the people. They came and began to work on the house of the LORD Almighty, their God, on the twenty-fourth day of the sixth month." [146]

When we tell our story, we describe the view from our vantage point on what the Author is doing in the cosmos, on where this whole thing might be going. The apostle Peter commanded us to always be ready to tell that story, truthfully and well, so that others will be drawn in and want to hear more. He told us to be "always be prepared to give an answer to everyone who asks you to give the reason for the hope that you have. But do this with gentleness and respect." [147]

Are you prepared to tell your story to anyone who asks?

- chapter 20 -

And They All Lived...

In Shakespeare's play *King Lear,* the Earl of Gloucester reflects on the chaos of life, about how arbitrary fate seems to be. He says, "As flies to wanton boys, are we to the gods. They kill us for their sport."[148]

In a world which cuts so many lives short before they get the resolution of a third act, pessimism is not unreasonable. Perhaps our belief that life is a story is just a narrative fallacy: we see a series of random events and imagine meaningful connections. Perhaps our lives are not stories connected to some larger purpose, and Thomas Hobbes was right when he said, "The life of man [is] solitary, poor, nasty, brutish, and short."[149] The Apostle Paul said much the same thing: "If there is no resurrection of the dead, then not even Christ has been raised. And if Christ has not been raised, our preaching is useless and so is your faith...If the dead are not raised, 'Let us eat and drink, for tomorrow we die.'"[150] Melancholy, rage, or the singular pursuit of pleasure—or all of them at once—are understandable responses to this life. We must choose to believe that our lives are God-given stories. But there are good reasons to make that choice, and most of the people who lived on this planet have done so.

If we are characters lost in the pages of our stories, then how do they end? What page are you on at this moment? Are you living through your chapter three, or forty-three? Are you in the beginning, middle, or near the end of your tale? It is hard not to think about it. As each day goes by, and the pages flip ever more quickly, we become increasingly aware that there will be a last page, and that we are getting closer to it.

What happens on the last page?

There have been plenty of suggestions. For the most part, the possible epilogues to life give few details, except that whatever it is keeps going, forever. Most of the world's religions imagine that the last page is carried on *ad infinitum:* we will pluck a harp on a fluffy cloud—forever; we will sing hymns in a celestial choir—forever; we will gaze endlessly on the face of God, our hearts full of love as the brightness of his glory blinds our eyes—forever; we will raise a mead horn in Valhalla, backslapping the other heroes and telling stories of our exploits—forever; seventy-two virgins will drop grapes in our mouth, in an endless loop—forever. In all these visions, and more, of the afterlife our stories hit a freeze frame, and then hold it infinitely. We gain eternity, but the narrative grinds to a halt; our character arcs completed. Based on this description, some of us worry that heaven might turn out to be a nice place—but kind of boring.

A few religions and philosophies have circular views of time, in which we are born, live, die, and are reborn again. Rinse and repeat, forever. On the other hand, our fate might rest in some equation about the mass and gravity of the cosmos, the universe expanding until all the dark matter slows it down enough for it to fall in on itself. Then it might bounce back out again in another Big Bang, the Dance of Shiva continuing through countless universes. Perhaps we are doomed to keep doing it over and over again until our essence grows enlightened enough to escape the cycle, into the endless, pleasant, and boring freeze frame of eternity.

None of us can prove that our expectation of the afterlife is true. We will all just have to conduct the ultimate experiment to find out who is right.

We experience our life stories as linear (they go in a timeline, from event to event) and meaningful (each event on our timeline is unique and connected to the whole). Perhaps this is just a trick of our perspective, a construct of our limited minds. But maybe not; it is, after all, the only way that we have ever known life to be. What if the afterlife is the same way? What if life goes on, from event to meaningful event, forever? In other words: what if our stories goes on, not just our souls?

Measured on the timeline of eternity, the rise and fall of empires are small things. They fill a page, perhaps a chapter—and then they are no more. The people who lived in them, however, go on forever. The buildings collapse, the borders disappear, the languages are forgotten. But the men and women who built, defended, and spoke—they are timeless beings. Their stories continue, and are important because they do. The chapters that are visible in this life are only the beginning of their character arcs. In their time here, they began to be who they are becoming. As C.S. Lewis said in his classic essay *The Weight of Glory,* "You have never talked to a mere mortal. Nations, cultures, arts, and civilizations—these are mortal, and their life is to ours as the life of a gnat. But it is immortals whom we joke with, work with, marry, snub, and exploit—immortal horrors or everlasting splendors."[151]

It is when we forget that we are immortal that this life is most puzzling. Why do the wicked prosper? Why do the just suffer? Why are innocent, young lives sometimes crushed with sorrows, or snuffed out before they flower? Why does the Author leave so many loose threads dangling? Should he not bring them together somehow, before the end? What about the billions of abrupt and unfinished endings throughout history? And not just unfinished lives, but unfinished business within them: creativity undeveloped, ideas not shared, dreams unexplored, loves without enough time to bear fruit. Are all of those to be left hanging?

Not if the last page is not the last page.

Knowing that we are immortal does not always satisfy us. We are used to short stories: news articles, television commercials, two-hour films, and four-hundred-page novels. We like it when the sportscaster recaps a three-and-a-half hour game in sixty seconds. It gets to the good parts quickly, dropping the boring stuff. We are impatient; we want the Author to unfold our lives and get to the point quickly, like the characters in Bible stories. We do not stop to think that the events that we run through during a ser-

mon or a Sunday school lesson took decades, or even generations, to unfold in real life. Those events were not quick
for those who lived through them. What we want are long
short stories—that is, we want the easy arc and quick resolution of a short story, but we want it to last forever. We
shudder to think that what frustrates us now might take a
very long time to resolve, or that our questions might not
get answered anytime soon. Even if we know that we are
lost in the pages of a long book, we do not necessarily like
it.

It is when we forget that we are immortal that our stories seem most at odds with the cosmos. If we are just mo-
mentary sparks, blowing in the winds of time, then we are
irrelevant. Then we truly are at the mercy of forces beyond
us, unconscious and uncaring. Then our demand for meaning is arrogant and impudent. The physicist Richard Feynman said, "It doesn't seem to me that this fantastically
marvelous universe, this tremendous range of time and
space and different kinds of animals, and all the different
planets, and all these atoms with all their motions, and so
on, all this complicated thing can merely be a stage so that
God can watch human beings struggle for good and evil—which is the view that religion has. The stage is too big
for the drama."[152] Feynman would be right—*if* we were
mortal.

Because we are not, this life is only momentarily puzzling. We are lost in the pages, but that does not mean that
the loose threads in our stories will not get wrapped up, or
that our tales will not fill the stage. If our narratives are
woven together into bigger stories, and finally into a Big

Story, then perhaps we will need a bigger stage and more time.

That seems to be exactly what God has in mind: to make a bigger stage.

Why is it that when we think of heaven, we imagine it to be smaller than this world? We may not have considered its dimensions, but when most people talk about it they do not make it sound very big. God will be sitting on a great throne, there will be a huge crowd standing around it, there will be a New Jerusalem,[153] a lake of fire, and not much else. Granted, that is all that the Bible describes, and it would be foolish to speculate beyond that. Even our personal descriptions seem rather limited: we will dwell in the New Jerusalem, singing worship songs—and not much else.

Revelation 21 tells us that God is going to make a new heaven and a new earth. I do not pretend to understand what it is going to be like, because some aspects are downright confusing. There will no longer be a sun or a moon: does that mean there will be no more solar systems? There will no longer be any sea, but there will be a lake of fire. Yet the Big Story seems to keep getting bigger: from Eden to Israel, from the Cross to the ends of the earth. As C.S. Lewis said, "Once a stable held something bigger than the whole world."[154] In the New Jerusalem the Tree of Life bears a new crop every month for the healing of the nations. The Author seems to be widening the Story. Why would he not broaden the stage as well? The cosmos is in labor pains, waiting for the children of God to grow up so that it can give birth to something. I assume that it will be grand, something big enough to hold whatever happens next.

Perhaps that is why people have always been drawn to art or stories that remind us that reality is bigger than what is visible from our page. Beethoven's *Ode to Joy,* or Van Gogh's *Starry Night,* give us chills because they remind us that there is more than this, and at any moment it might break through. Fairy tales do the same thing. Every culture has told and treasured them, though they have often been called by other names. They have no particular time or place, because they occur in a sort of parallel universe which might be all around us: a child goes into a wood and meets an elf, a woman's cat warns her of danger, a fisherman is instructed by a talking fish. The cosmos is more complicated than we suppose. We ride on the surface of this world, only rarely catching snatches of the deep vibrations still reverberating from the words the Author spoke when he set the creation into motion.

That is what the sacraments are: places where God punches a hole in space-time and the light of eternity shines through. Christ's death and resurrection have spread forward and backward through the Big Story. It changes everything, everywhere, in every time. It is part of yesterday, tomorrow, and forever. The Author wrote himself onto every page. The sacraments remind us that we are born banished from Eden, but that the Author entered his Story to reconcile himself to the lost.[155] He rips the fabric of the cosmos to bring the exiles home.

Maybe reconciliation is the reason the Author chooses to tell our lives as stories. The Author wants to align all things with his own heart. But how could we understand his heart? Novelists learn to show the character of their characters, not to tell the reader about it. Perhaps he could have expressed himself in some other way: through a divine, endless sermon or worship service. But not everything can be understood by those means. Perhaps God did not want to just tell the universe about himself, he wanted to *show* it who he is. How would you explain love, or goodness, or joy, or sacrifice, or nobility, or servanthood, or courage, or creativity, or genius—or anything else really worth knowing about God—without illustrating it through a story? Maybe that is the point of it all: maybe all our stories, and stories we have not even heard yet, are the biggest gift ever given. Something to delight us, to teach us, to grow us up, and to make us laugh and cry—all of those at the same time during some chapters. Something that will show us his heart and draw us toward it. Perhaps the Story is a gift to a cosmic audience composed of humans and angels and who knows what else. All will watch, listen, and learn who the Author is. They will hang on every word he speaks. Someday the cosmos will gasp and say, "Yes! Yes! And then what happened? And what happens next?"

God's words bring life. The first thing he does in Genesis is speak. His breath brought life. His words became a world. In the first chapter of John we learn that Christ himself is a word, the Word, who became flesh in his tale. The words of the Word are the stuff of our universe. In our day and age, we do not listen. We know so much about how things happen that we have given up really asking why they do. We know what things are made of, but not much about what they are. We think a lot about this life, but almost nothing about the next.

Do we really believe in eternal life? Then we are immortal. If we are immortal, then a trillion years from now our stories will just be getting started.

This life—that we wonder and worry so much about—is just the first sentence of the first paragraph on the first page of the longest, most complex, and surprising novel ever written. Of course your life does not make sense—yet. Of course you do not understand what is happening, or why. Be patient. Pay attention. See how this thing turns out. Be careful about who you are becoming. The shape of your eternal character arc is forming.

As the last stanza of the hymn *Amazing Grace* reminds us,

> When we've been there
> Ten thousand years
> Bright, shining as the sun
> We've no less days
> To sing God's praise
> Then when we first begun

Not only will be have no less days to sing God's praise, we'll have no less days to do all sorts of things and to continue to live this magnificent gift of a story. Ten thousand years? Ten *trillion* from now, we will still be forever young.

About the Author

Gregory Smith is a freelance writer, editor, and graphic designer. He is also a teaching pastor at Manna Vintage Faith, and speaks at churches, conferences, and colleges.

Greg and his wife Linda live with their children in Holland, Michigan.

Contact him through his website:
www.smithgreg.com

Acknowledgements

Linda, the stuff in this book is the fruit of our story. I would never have learned or written it without you. Thank you for being my best friend, and the best thing that ever happened to me. I thank God every day that we get to keep turning the pages together.

Andrew and Maggie, everyday the two of you inspire me to get up, write, and thank the Lord for my life. You are God's greatest grace to me. When all else seems uncertain, believe the Big Story, tell it to others, and let the Author shape your tale.

Mom and Dad, you believe(d) in me, to excess. I'm not really half as clever as you think, but you made me think I was clever enough to keep trying. But that's what parents are supposed to do. Thank you for everything.

Rod and Laura, when I sat on your deck that afternoon (with dysentery) and asked to marry your daughter, you asked what I would be when I grew up. I said that I was going to write. Sorry it took so long. Thanks for saying, "Yes," and for patient support along the way.

Manna Vintage Faith Community, thank you for your love, support, and encouragement over the years. And thanks for being guinea pigs (crash test dummies?) for developing some of this material. What we've done together has been the best thing I'll ever be a part of in ministry.

Dale and Annette, thanks for letting me think out loud about this stuff until the wee hours in your house(s) over the last twenty-five years, and for always being a home away from home. I expect my goddaughter and her beautiful sisters to read this book thoroughly.

Barbara, thanks for being my Barnabas, my Jiminy Cricket, and Tigger to my Eeyore. Don't mess with Texas, and really don't mess with Barbara. Linda and I have our reservations in for the compound.

Rob, thanks for pushing me to hurry up and and finish this one so I can move on to other projects, and for your help in turning this into a career.

Nate and Caitlin, thank you for your careful reading of the manuscript, catching so many of my innumerable errors, and your helpful suggestions. Any mistakes in this book are my own fault.

Notes

1 1 Corinthians 9:24; Galatians 2:2; Galatians 5:7; Hebrews 12:1 (all Bible quotations are from the New International Version).

2 In literature, the term *character arc* refers to the ways that a character changes—in personality, perspective, ideology, emotional maturity, loyalties, etc.—over the course of a story. If those changes were plotted on a graph, they would reveal a trajectory, or arc, over time. That arc describes the shape of the character's emerging identity.

3 For example, Psalm 51 explains that King David wrote it as a lament after the prophet Nathan exposed his adultery with Bathsheba and the murder of her husband to hide the deed.

4 As a convenience, I will capitalize the term "Author" in this book whenever I am referring to God in his role as the creator and director of everything that is, and all that happens (Acts 17:26-28).

5 In Jeremiah 29:11 God mentions the plans he has for us. That passage refers to God's intentions for what he will bring about during a later chapter in Israel's history. An author may very well have a plan for how he will develop the plot. That is not a set of hoops the characters have to jump through so that the author will shape the plot to their liking. In fact, the point of the passage is that God is going to bring his people back from Babylon, regardless of their actions. We should be leery of descriptions of God's plan for this or that. It is not that they are too ambitious, but that they lack imagination. God is usually surprising; Aslan is not a tame lion. Our predictions rob us of the wonder and the mystery that is obvious to anyone who is paying attention to the Bible and the world around us.

6 Genesis 3:5

7 Romans 8:19-22

8 Revelation 22:2

[9] For convenience, I will use the capitalized term "Big Story" to refer to the total movement of the created universe from its beginning to wherever the Author is taking it.

[10] *Cosmos: A Personal Voyage,* created by Carl Sagan, Ann Druyan, Steven Soter. Produced by PBS and KCET in 1978-79, first shown on PBS in 1980.

[11] Ibid., Episode 9, *The Lives of Stars*

[12] William Shakespeare, *As You Like It* (Act II, Scene VII), 1623

[13] Homer, *The Iliad,* Book XX. Translated by Samuel Butler.

[14] Interestingly, those first couple of chapters in Genesis and the last couple of chapters in Revelation, told from the perspective of the omniscient narrator, are the framing elements of the Big Story.

[15] Just to confuse anyone who has studied both philosophy and film, in film studies this is called *diegetic music,* using the term in the opposite way than Plato and Aristotle did.

[16] A bit of movie trivia: she never says, "Play it again, Sam."

[17] *Once,* written and directed by John Carney, starring (and music composed and performed by) Glen Hansard and Markéta Irglová, produced by Bórd Scannán na hÉireann (Irish Film Board), 2007

[18] Exodus 15:20-21

[19] Luke 1:46-55

[20] 2 Corinthians 12:2

[21] 1 Corinthians 13:12

[22] *Harper's,* August 1958

[23] Romans 5:18-19

[24] Romans 8:20-21

[25] John Milton, *Paradise Lost* (Book IX, lines 779-783), 1667

[26] 1 Corinthians 15:17-19; 32

[27] William Shakespeare, *Macbeth,* Act 5, Scene 5, 1623

Notes

28 Not racial in the sense of European or African or Asian races, but the human race.

29 Sigmund Freud, *Civilization and It's Discontents,* 1930

30 From *The Gay Science* (1882), in which Nietzsche first declared, "God is dead." The title refers to the joy he and other bohemian intellectuals felt at the waning influence of Christianity in late nineteenth century Europe.

31 François-Marie Arouet Voltaire, in a letter to Prince Frederick William of Prussia (1770), translated by S.G. Tallentyre, *Voltaire in His Letters,* 1919

32 Romans 1:19-20

33 Hebrews 12:1

34 Romans 8:19

35 Job 1:3

36 Job 1:1

37 Job 1:13-19

38 Job 2:7-8

39 Job 2:10

40 In several passages, the Bible alludes to (but never explains) something that resembles a supernatural council, a divine royal court (Genesis 1; Isaiah 6; Job 1-2, 38:7; 1 Kings 22:19-22). God is obviously the king, and head of this council, and angelic beings seem to be the courtiers and advisors. What is puzzling is that in at least two of these passages it appears that Satan or the rebellious angels have some access to the court. We do not know any more than that; apparently the Author did not think the details of God's throne room are relevant to our story.

41 Job 1:6-11

42 This story is told in the ninth chapter of the Gospel of John.

43 John 9:3

44 1 Corinthians 2:7

[45] This story is told in Exodus chapter 16. Note that God provided daily sources of protein (quails) and carbohydrate (manna) to sustain the people.

[46] Matthew 6:25-34

[47] This is a true story. Simon Stylites (390-459 AD) lived in Syria under the Byzantine Christian Empire, and is recognized as a saint by the Roman Catholic, Eastern Orthodox, and Oriental Orthodox Churches. He was one of the most famous and inspirational Christian leaders of his day.

[48] This is also a true story. The monastery of beehive huts perches on top of *Skellig Michael* ("St. Michael's Rock" in Gaelic), twelve miles off the westernmost point of Ireland. Today it is a UNESCO World Heritage site, visited only by tourists lucky enough to get a boat ride on a calm sea. From the seventh through the twelfth centuries it was occupied by a monastic community devoted to prayer, inspired by pioneers like Simon Stylites.

[49] Although this era spanned more than a thousand years of Church history, through far more generations than our contemporary church trends.

[50] Please see chapter thirteen for more discussion of our freedom within the Story.

[51] Thomas Aquinas, *Summa Theologica* (Treatment of the Cardinal Virtues, Question 83), 1274

[52] Luke 18:1-8

[53] In truth, almost everyone really believes this, even in a society that claims to be morally subjective.

[54] Romans 8:26

[55] Matthew 6:9-13

[56] The term comes from screenwriting more than novel writing. The term was coined during the golden age of Hollywood, although no one seems to know for sure where it came from or why it was called the MacGuffin. A producer would want to shoot some genre film, and order up a script. The writers would invent a MacGuffin to give the characters some reason to be onscreen. The same technique, if not the term, is used in novels and other forms of storytelling.

[57] Percy Bysshe Shelley, *Ozymandias,* 1819

[58] Matthew 28:20

[59] *The Confessions of Saint Augustine, Bishop of Hippo,* Book 1, Chapter 1, 398 AD

[60] Howard, Thomas, *Christ the Tiger: A Postscript to Dogma,* 1967

[61] For more about joy, see chapter eighteen.

[62] Psalm 37:4

[63] Isaiah 53:3

[64] Genesis 10:4

[65] Exodus 20:5-6

[66] Ibid.

[67] Genesis 22:17-18

[68] His son Ishmael (conceived with his servant Hagar) became the patriarch of nomadic peoples that are said to have become the Arabs (there is some question about whether the modern Arabs descended from this line). His younger son Isaac became the patriarch of people that would become the Jews. The history of the conflicts between the Jews and the nomadic peoples to the south and east of Israel has its roots in this family drama.

[69] Isaiah 49:15-17

[70] Esther 4:13-14

[71] Acts 13:36

[72] Matthew 25:21

73 Predestination is the doctrine that God has already determined everything that will happen, including our thoughts, choices, and eternal destiny.

74 Astrology asserts that the movements of the planets influence—or even determine—our personalities, choices, and even historical events. Some of those who scoff at the idea of God's predestination read their horoscope each day to learn whether they will fall in love or should avoid traveling—all because Jupiter aligned with Mars.

75 Another way to say this is that because God is outside time, there is no "future" for him. He sees the whole timeline from above, and from that vantage point he can see where things are going.

76 Matthew 18:6

77 Colossians 1:20

78 Luke 16:19-31

79 Matthew 22:1-14

80 Matthew 21:33-46. The immediate application of this parable is the Pharisees and Israel, but in the broader context of the New Testament it has implications for the final judgment of all humanity.

81 Luke 13:6-9

82 Mark 9:43-49

83 Matthew 8:28-29. It is clear from the context that the demons inhabiting these men ask this question. Jesus casts the demons out. But "the appointed time" is an ominous foreshadow of things to come.

84 There are several words in Hebrew and Greek that are translated into the English word "hell." Some mean the place where the dead go to await resurrection and judgment. Others imply a place of punishment. The examples I am citing in this chapter are of the second type.

85 2 Peter 2:4-9

[86] Romans 9:14-16

[87] Romans 9:17-18

[88] Exodus 5:1-3. At first, Moses did not ask Pharaoh to set the Hebrews free, only to grant them a religious holiday. When Pharaoh refused, God raised the stakes.

[89] Romans 9:20-21

[90] Romans 9:22-23

[91] Revelation 21:4

[92] Sermon LXVI, *Devotions Upon Emergent Occasions,* 1624

[93] Ibid.

[94] John Milton, *Paradise Lost* (Book I, lines 262-263), 1667

[95] Ibid., lines 253-255

[96] Ibid., Book IV, lines 107-109

[97] Ephesians 6:11-12

[98] Ephesians 2:2

[99] John 8:44

[100] 1 Peter 5:8

[101] Stephen Crane wrote *The Red Badge of Courage* in 1895. A short work, it is among the most celebrated of American novels, recording an engagement that resembles the Battle of Chancellorsville from the Union perspective.

[102] Ernest Hemingway wrote *The Old Man and the Sea* in Cuba in 1951. Also a short novel, it has become a modern classic.

[103] With no omniscient narrator, we only learn what the young man learns. He never knows exactly where he is or what is going on around him on the larger battlefield—much the way that we experience life.

[104] Romans 7:15-24

[105] Genesis 3:17-19

[106] Matthew 6:25-34

[107] Psalm 23:4

[108] Romans 6:23

[109] 1 Peter 5:8-9

[110] Revelation 12:10

[111] Matthew 8:27

[112] John 1:1

[113] Colossians 1:15-17

[114] Genesis 15

[115] Genesis 18

[116] 1 Kings 19

[117] Daniel 3

[118] Isaiah 53:3

[119] Romans 5:14

[120] 1 Corinthians 15:26

[121] Psalm 68 foretold it, and Paul confirms it in Ephesians 4:8

[122] If this sounds suspiciously like Tolkien's *The Lord of the Rings*, it is because J.R.R. Tolkien was a professor of early Germanic-English literature, and he and Wagner were both influenced by many of the same myths and sagas.

[123] 2 Corinthians 12:7-10

[124] See chapter twelve for more thoughts about the heartbreaks of life.

[125] Romans 8:20-21

[126] See chapter four for more discussion of how the cosmos has been affected by sin.

[127] 2 Corinthians 12:7

[128] Song of Solomon 2:1

Notes

[129] Among other things, he asks, "What, exactly, makes a movie 'Christian?'"

[130] The story of Abram (who was renamed 'Abraham') and Sarah runs through Genesis chapters 12-25.

[131] The story of Joseph and his brothers is told in Genesis chapters 37-50.

[132] The story of Hannah is told in 1 Samuel, chapter 1.

[133] Acts 3

[134] John 8

[135] Luke 7

[136] John 13:23; 19:26; 20:2; 21:7; 21:20; Revelation 1

[137] Revelation 22:2

[138] Charles Frazier, *Cold Mountain,* Vintage Books Contemporary Edition, 1998, page 308

[139] René Descartes, *Meditations on First Philosophy,* 1641. The actual phrase he used, "I am, I exist," came to be popularly paraphrased as "I think, therefore I am."

[140] Genesis 3:7-8

[141] Genesis 4:9

[142] Sir Walter Scott, Marmion (Canto VI, XVII), 1808

[143] Ezra 3:7-8

[144] Ezra 3:11-13

[145] Zechariah 4:6

[146] Haggai 1:14-15

[147] 1 Peter 3:15

[148] William Shakespeare, *King Lear,* Act IV, Scene 1

[149] Thomas Hobbes, *Leviathan,* 1651

[150] 1 Corinthians 15:13-14; 32

[151] C.S. Lewis, *The Weight of Glory* (first delivered as an address at Oxford University in 1941), Harper Collins, 1980

[152] Statement (1959), quoted by James Gleick in *Genius: The Life and Science of Richard Feynman* (1992)

[153] Revelation 21:15-17 describes the New Jerusalem as a cube approximately the size of earth's moon. That is a huge city, and the dimensions are probably symbolic, meant to suggest that it is big enough to contain more than we can imagine.

[154] C.S. Lewis, *The Last Battle* (*The Chronicles of Narnia*), Harper Collins, 1956.

[155] 2 Corinthians 5